THE THINKING EDGE

HOW TO RECLAIM THE MINDSET THAT MACHINES CAN'T COPY

This isn't a book about artificial intelligence.
It's a book about authentic intelligence.

ANNABELEN HEMELGARN

CONTENTS

AUTHOR'S NOTE
HOW THIS BOOK WAS BORN

It began on an ordinary evening, the kind that doesn't ask to be remembered.

Sidebar

Reflection Lab: The First Crack

- What parts of your work or identity feel uncertain right now?
- What emotion come up when you think about change—fear, frustration, or curiosity?
- What's one small "crack" you've been ignoring that might actually be an invitation to grow?

In the rush to automate, don't forget the miracle that can't be coded: your capacity to think.

My father-in-law, Jim, and I were sitting in his living room, the hum of a football game in the background, when he reached for the remote, paused the screen, and said quietly, "I don't know where people fit anymore."

He wasn't asking me for an answer—he was naming something true.

A quiet ache shared by many who've worked hard, built something solid, and suddenly find the world moving faster than they ever imagined.

That moment stayed with me.

Because underneath his words was a deeper question—one I'd been circling in my own work and life:

Where do we, as humans, still belong when the world seems to be run by machines?

But now, the world is sprinting ahead, powered by code.

Machines THINK faster, process more, never sleep.

And if you've ever woken up at 2 a.m. wondering where you fit in that equation, you're not alone.

Technology was supposed to free us. Instead, it exposed us.

It forced a new question: *What's left when everything else can be automated?*

That question is where this book begins.

Because the cracks aren't collapse—they're clarity. They reveal what we've built on autopilot, and they invite us to rebuild with intention.

In a time when the world is accelerating, the real revolution belongs to those who can slow down long enough to THINK.

Over the years, I've watched businesses grow, pivot, and disappear. I've seen people burn out chasing speed, and others come back to life the moment they started thinking differently again.

What I've learned is simple, but not easy: the real danger isn't automation—it's autopilot.

The Thinking Edge is my invitation to wake up your mind again—to rediscover the quiet strength that comes from awareness, imagination, and faith.

THE THINK FRAMEWORK

Somewhere along this journey, a rhythm began to form—a way to navigate change without losing yourself in it.

It's neither a formula nor a theory; rather, it's a pattern I noticed in my own pivots and in the people and companies that thrived while others froze.

That rhythm became **THINK.**

It's not something to memorize; it's something to embody.

T—Tell the Truth

See where you truly are. Identify what's working and what isn't—without denial or judgment.

H—Harness Your Imagination

Curiosity is courage in disguise. Allowing yourself to wonder again lets vision take shape.

I—Identify Your Human Edge

Discover what no machine can replicate—empathy, discernment, creativity, and faith. These are your differentiators.

N—Navigate the Noise

The world is loud. Learning to listen for what truly matters is the new superpower.

K—Keep Moving

Clarity without motion is still drift. Action—small, steady, intentional—is how you keep your mind awake.

This is the heartbeat of the book.

Each part invites you to think a little deeper, see a little clearer, and act with increased intention—not to compete with machines, but to become more fully human in a world that's forgotten how.

Before we can imagine what's next, we must be honest about where we are.

The first step in thinking differently is often the hardest—acknowledging the truth about where we've been drifting.

Every transformation begins with truth—not the polished version we present to others, but the quiet kind that asks hard questions in the mirror. *Tell the Truth* is the first step back to awareness.

It's where drifting ends and thinking begins—the moment you choose clarity over comfort and begin to see, with open eyes, what's truly shaping your life, your work, and your mind.

PART I

T: TELL THE TRUTH — WAKE UP TO THE DRIFT

CHAPTER 1
THE GROUND SHIFT

A Night on the Couch

It started on an ordinary evening. My father-in-law, Jim, and I were sitting in his living room, the TV quietly playing the latest football game when he began discussing AI and the future of work. He reached for the remote, paused the screen, and said, almost to himself, "I don't know where people fit anymore."

Jim is eighty-three; we had this discussion in 2024. For decades, he managed retail stores for a company called **SCOA—The Shoe Company of America**. That name no longer exists; the company folded in 2002, long before the rise of chatbots or self-driving cars. Yet Jim still remembers the smell of new leather when a shipment arrived, the rhythm of folding tissue paper into boxes, and the pride of hitting monthly sales targets.

He built a life on hard work, loyalty, and handshakes—values that once guaranteed stability. Yet as he absently watched the game, a flicker of uncertainty appeared in his eyes.

"It's not me I'm worried about," he said. "It's my grandkids. How are they going to build a career if everything's done by machines?"

His question hung in the air. It wasn't rhetorical; it was generational.

The Quiet Panic of Progress

I understood exactly what he meant. I've lived through multiple reinventions myself.

I began as a process engineer—trained at Purdue to think in systems, formulas, and precision. Later, I earned a master's in digital marketing through the University of Cincinnati's DAAP program, drawn to the psychology of creativity and consumer behavior.

My career started in marketing through freelancing and entrepreneurship, but the 2008 financial collapse forced a reckoning. When marketing budgets were cut almost immediately, it became clear that this wasn't a failure of skill—it was a shift in economic reality.

We had to rethink where value lived.

The move into the energy industry wasn't a leap—it was a logical extension of systems thinking. Advertising may be optional in a downturn, but energy is not. People delay spending, but they don't stop flipping the lights on. That insight shaped the pivot—not fear, but foresight.

Each time I built something solid, the market shifted. Each time I adapted, the world redefined the rules faster.

My energy business reached seven figures—even as automation transformed what once required a team into software. My marketing agency thrived—until AI tools began producing results in *minutes* that used to take *months*.

It's breathtaking how quickly "value" changes definition.

Yet, amid all that acceleration, one thing remains constant: **humans still choose what matters.**

When Thinking Stops, Giants Fall

I pondered Jim's question long after that night. What happens when people—or companies—stop thinking?

It's easy to say "disruption" killed Blockbuster, but that's not entirely true. **Denial did.**

In the early 2000s, Netflix offered to partner with Blockbuster. Blockbuster laughed them out of the room. Why? Because their entire identity was built on *what had worked*. Rows of blue-and-yellow stores, late fees, Friday nights at the checkout counter—*nostalgia disguised as a business model.*

Meanwhile, Netflix kept thinking. They recognized where technology was heading. They experimented, iterated, and embraced uncertainty.

Two decades later, Netflix became a verb. Blockbuster became a punchline.

Technology didn't destroy them. Complacent thinking did. They stopped imagining, questioning, and innovating.

Jim nodded when I shared that story.

"I remember those stores," he said quietly. "Every town had one." He leaned back in his chair. "Guess that's what happens when you THINK you're too big to change."

That, right there, is the first truth of this book: **Survival belongs to the THINKers, not the reactors.**

The Drift We Don't See

Most of us aren't that different from Blockbuster. We build comfortable routines, rely on familiar strategies, and mistake motion for progress. Then one day, we realize we've drifted.

Drifting doesn't announce itself. It doesn't surface as a crisis. It manifests as routine. It looks like:

- Doing what you've always done "because it used to work."
- Dismissing new tools instead of learning to use them.
- Complaining about change instead of engaging with it.
- Confusing busyness with intention.

The opposite of drifting isn't hustling harder—it's **thinking deliberately**.

Thinking isn't just analysis; it's awareness. It's that quiet moment when you ask, *"Where am I, really? And where is this heading?"*

That's what Jim was doing on his couch that night. He was thinking—truly thinking—about the future. In that humility, he was already ahead of most people.

What Machines Still Can't Do

Machines can replicate processes. They can predict patterns, sort data, and even mimic emotion. But they can't create *meaning*. They can't imagine purpose. They can't decide what matters most.

That's your job. That's your human edge—the part no machine can imitate.

Every leap forward in history—every revolution, invention, and movement—began with someone asking a better question. AI will only amplify those who know how to do that.

When you stop thinking, you hand over your agency. When you start thinking again, you reclaim your future.

The Real Question

So here's the question I'll ask you, the same one that's been echoing in my mind:

"What are you doing with your mind?"

Not your degree, title, or skill set—your *mind.*

That is your only irreplaceable asset. Everything else—data, formulas, code—can be replicated.

Your ability to reason, imagine, interpret, and create—those are divine gifts. The danger isn't that AI will take them; it's that we'll forget to use them.

The Promise of What's Ahead

This book is your invitation to THINK again. To stop drifting, start designing, and reclaim the creative muscle you were born with.

In the next chapters, we'll explore a framework called **THINK**:

- **Tell the Truth** – See your current reality without denial.

- **Harness Your Imagination** – Reconnect to vision and curiosity.

- **Identify Your Human Edge** – Know what makes you irreplaceable.

- **Navigate the Noise** – Develop discernment in an age of overload.

- **Keep Moving** – Turn clarity into courageous action.

Through real stories—people like Jim, professionals like you, and companies that thrived or faltered based on their thought processes—you'll learn how to pivot, adapt, and succeed.

Because the future doesn't belong to those who can predict it. It belongs to those who can **THINK** their way through it.

And that begins right here—with the courage to tell yourself the truth about where you stand.

CHAPTER 2
THE COMFORT TRAP

Most people don't notice they've stopped thinking—they just call it *experience*.

It happens quietly. You master a skill, land the promotion, and find your rhythm. You stop questioning the process because it worked. You begin repeating what made you successful, assuming it always will.

That's the trap.

Comfort disguised as competence is the beginning of decline.

Lena: The Creative Who Stopped Creating

Lena had been in marketing for nearly fifteen years. She was good—sharp instincts, a solid portfolio, the kind of professional people turned to when they needed effective campaigns. Her clients trusted her. Her team relied on her.

But lately, the world was changing faster than her playbook.

She'd open LinkedIn and see post after post about "AI-generated ad copy," "data-driven creative," and "chatbot brand voice systems." At first, she laughed it off—*those can't replace what I do.* Then she'd see clients repost those same tools with captions like, *"This could save our team hours!"*

The laughter got quieter.

One morning, she opened her laptop and stared at a campaign outline she'd written countless times before: product highlight, target audience, value proposition, CTA. It was fine; it was what she knew. But for the first time, she felt its emptiness.

She wasn't thinking anymore—just running on mental autopilot.

That's when she realized she was *drifting.*

She didn't hate her job. That was the problem—it was comfortable enough to silence the part of her that still wanted more.

Lena had built her career on consistency. Her marketing campaigns were predictable, profitable, and safe. Every Monday looked like the last—strategy decks, brand briefs, and coffee-fueled brainstorms that produced what clients expected.

Until one morning, her team used AI to build a campaign in thirty minutes that normally took two weeks. It worked, and the client was thrilled. But Lena wasn't.

Her first thought wasn't excitement; it was dread. If this tool could do her job faster, what did that mean for *her*?

That's when she realized: She wasn't just trapped in her job; she was trapped in her comfort.

The Drift Feels Safe... Until It's Not

Drifting never feels dangerous at first. It feels efficient, familiar, even successful.

It looks like:

- Repeating the same strategy because it worked once.
- Avoiding new tools because "we don't have time to learn that right now."
- Managing instead of imagining.
- Protecting the past instead of preparing for the future.

Lena didn't realize it yet, but she'd entered what I call **the comfort trap**—that invisible line between mastery and stagnation.

And she wasn't alone.

The Corporate Comfort Trap: Kodak

Once upon a time, *Kodak* was untouchable.

They owned photography. Their film defined an entire industry. Their tagline—*"Kodak moments"*—literally became part of human language.

Then, in 1975, a young engineer inside Kodak's lab invented something revolutionary: the digital camera. Kodak owned the patent and saw the future on their own desks.

But the executives dismissed it. Digital wasn't "on brand." It threatened their film profits. They didn't want to cannibalize what was working.

So they shelved the idea.

Decades later, other companies commercialized digital photography, and Kodak went bankrupt—holding the patent that could have saved them.

They didn't lose because of technology. They lost because of comfort. The system that once made them great became the system they were afraid to outgrow.

Sound familiar?

When Comfort Becomes Blindness

Lena didn't work for Kodak, but she was living the same story—different century, same psychology.

Every time she opened a new AI tool, she felt resistance tighten in her chest.

What if I don't understand it?

What if I use it wrong?

What if this makes me irrelevant?

So, she stayed in her lane. She did what she knew. And like Kodak, she mistook *doing things the old way* for *doing things the right way*.

But deep down, she knew the truth.

Her fear wasn't about learning new tools—it was about remembering how to think again.

That's the real danger of comfort: it tricks smart people into playing small.

The Lived Truth (Your Voice)

I'm not a psychologist. I'm not a researcher analyzing data points or case studies. I'm someone who has lived this—who has built thriving businesses and then watched them hit walls as the world evolved faster than my systems.

I've seen how quickly success can turn into complacency. I've learned that survival doesn't belong to the fastest or the loudest; it belongs to those who remain curious enough to keep thinking, even when it's uncomfortable.

That's why I'm writing this book—not to lecture you on theory, but to provide a way forward when the ground shifts beneath you.

You can't outwork what you refuse to outthink.

The Moment of Realization

One afternoon, Lena finally opened an AI platform she had been avoiding. She typed a prompt, hit enter, and within seconds watched her computer generate a campaign outline that used to take her a week.

Her stomach dropped.

She wasn't angry. She was awake.

Because that moment—the collision of fear and insight—is when *thinking begins again.*

If she could lean into that discomfort instead of away from it, she could rebuild herself stronger than ever.

That's what this chapter invites you to do.

The Drift Equation: Comfort → Complacency → Crisis

Every comfort zone has an expiration date. We rarely notice until it's too late.

Psychologist Carol Dweck's research on the *fixed mindset* shows that our desire to remain competent can prevent us from taking new risks. We protect what we know instead of evolving into what's next.

"The moment you stop stretching, you start drifting."

And drift is insidious. It doesn't announce itself. It quietly pulls you away from relevance—one repeated habit, one unchallenged idea at a time.

The Hidden Cost of Familiarity

Innovation expert Francesca Gino (Harvard Business Review) refers to it as *the familiarity trap*—the more we repeat what works, the less we notice what's changing.

Kodak had the patent for the digital camera but ignored it.

They didn't fail because they couldn't invent.

They failed because they didn't want to reinvent.

Lena recognized that same pattern in herself. She wasn't obsolete; she was *overly consistent*.

The Drift Audit™

To reclaim your thinking edge, you must identify where you've stopped using it.

Take a moment to conduct your own Drift Audit—five questions to reveal where comfort has quietly become your ceiling.

1. What areas of your work or life feel repetitive but "safe"?
2. What tools or ideas have you dismissed without truly exploring?
3. What problems have you stopped trying to solve because you've accepted "that's just how it is"?
4. Where have you stopped asking *why*?
5. What would you lose if you actually grew beyond what's comfortable?

Write your answers. Be honest. Don't rush.

You can't change what you won't confront.

The Drift Audit (Mini Exercise)

Now rate yourself (1–5) in each area below:

1. Work habits—Am I experimenting or repeating?
2. Relationships—Do I ask new questions or replay old scripts?

3. Learning—When was the last time I learned something unrelated to my field?

4. Spiritual life—Do I pause, reflect, and listen, or just perform routines?

Scores:

- 4–5 → You're growing.
- 2–3 → You're coasting.
- 1 → You're drifting.

Awareness brings us back. It reveals choices we didn't even realize we were making.

From Comfort to Clarity

The opposite of comfort isn't chaos; it's clarity.

When you start thinking again—when curiosity replaces fear—you see new angles, connections, and futures. That's how Netflix embraced streaming while others clung to DVD rentals. That's how innovators like Lena pivot before market forces compel them to.

Change isn't coming someday; it's here now.

But so is your mind.

So is your ability to think, imagine, and choose differently.

Comfort might feel safe, but safety is an illusion.

The only real security you'll ever have is your ability to think your way forward.

CHAPTER 3
FACING REALITY WITH FAITH

When everything you know begins to shift, faith becomes more than belief—it becomes focus.

In engineering, we learned that every system under pressure either cracks or reconfigures.

The same is true for people.

Crisis doesn't destroy character; it reveals it.

The old rules of success—hard work, seniority, predictability—are being rewritten.

So what do you hold onto when the formula fails?

Faith.

Not blind optimism or wishful thinking.

Faith as focused awareness.

A steady mind that refuses to panic.

Psychiatrist Viktor Frankl, who survived Nazi concentration camps, wrote that the last human freedom is the power "to choose one's attitude in any given set of circumstances."

That choice—not your title or technology—is what makes you irreplaceable.

The Myth of Security

For most of us, security is a story we were taught to believe.

Do the right things, follow the steps, and life will unfold in order: school, degree, job, success.

I believed that too.

Engineering school at Purdue taught me logic, formulas, and systems. I learned to solve problems efficiently—as long as they fit within the equation. But I didn't realize that the most important problems in life don't come with clear variables.

They appear as questions like:

"Who am I when everything I built no longer works?" "How do I lead when I don't even know what the next rule is?"

No one teaches you that in school.

Our education system trains memory, not mastery.

We were conditioned to memorize answers, not to question the system that created the test. Now, when the test itself changes daily, most people freeze.

We're rewarded for regurgitating the "right" answer, not for questioning whether the question even makes sense.

We've built a culture of copy-paste thinking—efficient, predictable, obedient.

Now, in an age where AI can memorize faster, compute better, and regurgitate more flawlessly than any of us, we're realizing how fragile that model truly is.

Because if you only know how to repeat, you've already been replaced.

The Erosion of Thinking

You can feel it everywhere.

People don't *pause* anymore; they scroll, consume, and react.

Social media isn't just shaping what we see—it's shaping *how we THINK*.

The algorithms aren't designed to enlighten you—they're designed to *own your attention*.

— If you seek joy, you'll find joy.
— If you seek outrage, you'll encounter outrage.

— If you're lost and drifting, you'll see that drifting is normal—that scrolling is self-care, that distraction is rest, that sameness is safety.
— If you're sad, you'll experience sadness.
— If you're angry, you'll encounter outrage.
— If you're drifting, you'll be surrounded by other drifters.

The algorithm doesn't care about your growth—it only cares that you stay.

That's not harmless; it's hypnotic.

We are conditioned to confuse stimulation with reflection, validation with growth.

And the scariest part?

We've stopped noticing.

The more time we spend in the feed, the less time we spend in thought. And when thinking dies, humanity drifts.

The Engineer's Reality Check

I've been there too.

I've stared at dashboards full of numbers, engagement rates, and performance charts—all the metrics that were supposed to indicate whether I was "winning."

But here's the truth no one tells you: numbers can't measure purpose.

You can hit every KPI and still feel completely lost.

You can appear successful on paper and know deep down you've stopped growing.

That realization—the quiet, gut-deep one—is where faith begins.

Faith isn't pretending everything's fine—it's the courage to face reality and move forward. It's looking directly at instability and saying, "I will not drift. I will learn. I will THINK my way forward."

That's what this chapter is about—not blind optimism, but informed belief.

IBM: Reinventing the Impossible

When people talk about "reinvention," they usually picture startups—fast, agile, new. But one of the most enduring examples of reinvention didn't come from a startup; it came from IBM, one of the oldest technology companies on earth.

Founded in 1911, IBM has reinvented itself multiple times—from mechanical tabulators to mainframes, from hardware to software, from computers to cloud. Each time the market shifted, IBM could have doubled down on what it knew. It could have been Kodak.

Instead, it kept thinking.

It asked hard questions:

"Where are we drifting?" "What business are we really in?" "What do we need to become next?"

In 1993, when IBM faced near collapse, the company brought in a new CEO, Lou Gerstner, who famously said,

"The last thing IBM needs right now is a vision."

He meant that before they could dream again, they had to face reality first—acknowledge where they were, what was broken, and why the old playbook no longer worked.

That brutal honesty saved them.

They downsized hardware, focused on consulting, embraced cloud computing, and later AI with Watson.

IBM didn't survive on faith alone.

It survived because it had faith in motion—the kind that partners with truth.

That's the same kind of faith this chapter asks of you.

Faith in Practice

Faith isn't passive.

It's not waiting for things to improve.

It's choosing to act on what you believe is possible before you can prove it.

That's what separates those who drift from those who rise.

When I pivoted industries—from engineering to marketing to energy to digital—I wasn't fearless; I was faithful. I trusted that clarity would follow movement, not precede it.

The future doesn't reveal itself to those who wait for certainty; it reveals itself to those who embrace intentional uncertainty.

You can't see the entire map, and you don't need to.

You just need to take the next step and trust your mind to meet you there.

Faith in motion is more powerful than fear in theory.

Reflection: Where Am I Pretending the Old Rules Still Work?

Let's get real.

Each of us has areas where we cling to the past—not because it's better, but because it's familiar.

Take a quiet moment and answer honestly:

- Where in your work or business are you following a rule that no longer makes sense?
- What belief are you holding onto simply because it's "how it's always been done"?
- What system, habit, or strategy are you protecting even though it keeps you small?
- What truth are you avoiding because it would require change?

Write your answers. Don't overthink them.

Clarity begins when honesty replaces illusion.

The 3R Model: Recognize → Reframe → Respond

When reality shifts:

- **Recognize** what's changing—name the fear honestly.
- **Reframe** it as data, not doom—what is this moment teaching you?
- **Respond** with alignment—act on your values, not your panic.

This is how IBM survived three major reinventions.

They didn't predict the future; they recognized reality, reframed their business, and responded with courage.

Reflection Exercise: Faith in Uncertainty

Ask yourself:

- Where am I pretending the old rules still work?
- What is this disruption revealing about my resilience?
- What would it look like to trust that even in uncertainty, there's an invitation?

As Daniel Kahneman explains in Thinking, Fast and Slow, our brains default to "System 1"—reactive, fast, habitual. Faith invites us back into "System 2"—slow, reflective, deliberate.

Faith gives you the strength to pause—and thinking happens in that pause.

The Bridge to What's Next

Lena's story was about waking up.

Jim's was about remembering what matters.

Yours is about reclaiming control—over your mind, your choices, and the direction of your future.

The world is changing. Fast. But so can you.

You don't need a PhD in psychology or a degree in futurism to adapt. You just need the courage to do what most people won't: **THINK for yourself.**

Faith isn't about ignoring fear—it's about refusing to let fear dictate your decisions.

In the next section, we'll explore how to discover the part of you that no algorithm can replicate—your Human Edge.

Because thinking differently begins with remembering that your mind is sacred ground.

And faith?

Faith is how you choose to keep it alive.

INTERLUDE: FAITH AS FOCUS
THE STILLNESS ADVANTAGE

The noise never stops.

Notifications, updates, headlines, chatter—each pulling at your attention like static on a signal.

We live in an era where speed is celebrated, but reflection is neglected.

We measure how quickly we respond rather than how deeply we understand.

We reward motion over meaning.

Deep down, everyone knows this truth:

You can't THINK clearly if you never stop moving.

The Overload Problem

MIT researchers found that the average professional now switches tasks every 47 seconds.

Each switch fractures focus, and every fracture drains energy.

Our devices—despite their brilliance—have trained us to confuse awareness with alertness. We're awake but not attentive.

We're scrolling but not absorbing.

We're connecting but not thinking.

And when your mind is constantly interrupted, your best ideas never arrive—they're drowned out by the noise.

But there's an antidote—one that predates technology and is simpler than any app: **stillness.**

The Power of Stillness

Stillness is not doing nothing; it's doing one thing with your whole mind.

It's the quiet before a decision, the breath before a response, the pause that transforms chaos into clarity.

When you practice stillness, you're not disconnecting from the world; you're reconnecting to yourself, to your thoughts, your values, and your sense of what truly matters.

This is where faith comes in—not as a religious doctrine but as a kind of trust.

Trust that you don't have to race every moment to matter.

Trust that clarity will emerge when you create space for it.

For some, that space appears through meditation or journaling.

For others, it's found in silence, nature, or quiet reflection.

It's not about the method; it's about the moment—the deliberate act of pausing long enough to THINK.

The Stillness Loop: Pause → Reflect → Perceive → Proceed

- Pause—Step away from the noise. Silence notifications, close the tab, or take a short walk.
- Reflect—Ask yourself one grounding question: What truly matters right now?
- Perceive—Notice what arises when the noise subsides— an idea, an emotion, a next step.
- Proceed—Move forward slowly but deliberately, aligned with what matters most.

This isn't weakness; it's leadership.

It's how modern innovators sustain clarity in chaos.

When Satya Nadella took over Microsoft, his first move wasn't acceleration—it was reflection.

He rebuilt the company's culture around empathy, curiosity, and listening.

That shift—from speed to stillness—sparked one of the greatest corporate turnarounds of the modern era.

Stillness, it turns out, isn't a retreat; it's a strategy.

The 5-Minute Stillness Practice

- Find a quiet space—even a parked car, a hallway, or a corner of your office will do.
- Set a timer for 5 minutes.
- Breathe in for 4 seconds, hold for 4, exhale for 6.
- Ask: "What's trying to get my attention right now?"
- Write down the first thought, word, or feeling that surfaces.

That's it.

You've just practiced the discipline of thinking.

Stillness isn't about escaping life—it's about returning to it awake.

"Stillness isn't silence. It's signal. It's where your best ideas begin to speak."

Closing Thought

If you want to think clearly, lead wisely, and live intentionally in an age that never slows down—you must be the one who slows down first.

Not to fall behind, but to see ahead.

Because clarity doesn't come from constant motion; it comes from deliberate stillness.

And the future belongs to those who can think deeply, act intentionally, and remain alert in a drifting world.

PART II

H: HARNESS YOUR IMAGINATION — DESIGN WHAT'S NEXT

CHAPTER 4
THE POWER OF POSSIBILITY

The day Lena watched a computer outthink her, she realized how limited her imagination had become.

She wasn't lazy or careless—she was simply stuck in a loop.

It was a Tuesday morning. Her coffee had gone cold beside her keyboard, and she was on her fourth draft of a social media campaign. She'd written versions of this same pitch countless times before: catchy hook, call to action, email follow-up.

Routine. Predictable. Safe.

Out of curiosity—or perhaps fatigue—she decided to test one of the AI tools her junior copywriter had mentioned. She typed in her campaign brief, hit enter, and watched.

In less than 30 seconds, the tool generated a full campaign. Not perfect, but polished enough to make her pause.

A pit formed in her stomach.

The first thought was fear: That's my job. The second was anger: How dare it be that good? The third was something different—something quieter and far more dangerous: What if I stopped competing with it and started thinking beyond it?

That's when fear began to give way to curiosity.

And curiosity is where imagination begins.

The Cost of Shrinking Vision

The problem isn't that technology is moving too fast.

It's that our imagination has stopped keeping pace.

We've spent so much time reacting, optimizing, and surviving that we've forgotten how to envision.

When you stop imagining, you start repeating.

And repetition, even when successful, is just a slower form of drift.

The truth is: most people don't fear failure—they fear imagination. Because imagination requires you to admit that the life you're living might be too small for who you're becoming.

That's where Lena found herself that morning—sitting in the tension between what she knew and what she could now envision.

The Netflix Moment

History is full of people and companies that reached the same crossroads.

In 2007, Netflix mailed DVDs in little red envelopes. Their model worked beautifully—millions of subscribers, predictable revenue, satisfied customers.

They could have remained comfortable.

But Reed Hastings saw something others didn't: the internet was becoming fast enough to stream. It was untested, expensive, and fraught with risk. But he imagined what could be, not just what was.

Blockbuster laughed.

Netflix built.

And the rest is legend.

Netflix didn't predict the future—they designed it.

That's what thinking does.

That's what imagination is for.

Every great pivot in history began not with data, but with a question:

"What if we're capable of more than this?"

That's the question this chapter is asking you.

The Engineering of Imagination

As an engineer, I once believed imagination was reserved for creatives—dreamers, artists, visionaries. People who lived in color while the rest of us dealt in blueprints.

I was wrong.

Imagination is simply the act of envisioning what doesn't exist yet. It's an engineering skill—one that builds ideas instead of machines.

Every innovation—from a bridge to a business—began as someone's unseen thought.

When you allow yourself to imagine, you activate the mental circuitry that transforms problems into patterns and chaos into concepts. It's the mechanism of design—for systems, companies, and lives.

So when I say **harness your imagination**, I'm not asking you to fantasize.

I'm asking you to design what's next.

Why Fear Fights Imagination

The moment you start envisioning a bigger future, fear inevitably appears.

The unknown threatens the comfortable.

Your old self—the one reliant on certainty—struggles with the concept of possibility.

Here's the paradox: fear and imagination engage the same brain muscle.

The only difference is the direction.

Fear envisions what could go wrong.

Imagination envisions what could go right.

The energy is identical—it's simply directed oppositely.

You can't eliminate fear, but you can retrain it.

Fear and growth cannot coexist—you must choose which one remains.

That's precisely what Lena did when she stopped resenting AI and began asking, "What could I create with this?"

That was her pivot.

Future Snapshot: The Exercise

Now it's your turn.

If imagination feels abstract, here's how to make it tangible.

Grab your journal and take five uninterrupted minutes. No phone. No noise. No multitasking.

Answer this prompt:

"If fear weren't a factor, what would I design next—in my work, my relationships, my life?"

Then, dive deeper:

- Where am I currently playing it safe?
- What's one bold idea I've dismissed as 'impractical'?
- What would my ideal day look like if I stopped reacting and started designing?
- Who would I need to become to make that vision possible?
- What first step could I take in the next 48 hours to move toward it?

This is your Future Snapshot. It's not fantasy—it's your blueprint in embryo.

Because imagination without intention is daydreaming.

But imagination with direction is strategy.

Faith, the Original Imagination

Faith and imagination are twins.

Faith says, "I can't see it yet, but I believe it's real."

Imagination says, "I can't see it yet, but I can picture how it might work."

When you combine them, you move from reaction to creation.

That's what this moment in history demands—not more productivity, not more optimization, but more vision. AI can build what exists.

Only humans can imagine what doesn't.

That's your divine assignment—to THINK, to dream, to design.

Lena learned that. Netflix proved it. And now it's your turn.

Closing Reflection

"Where in your life have you stopped imagining because you decided it was too late, too risky, or too unrealistic?"

Write it down.

Sit with it.

Then flip it: "What if it's exactly what I'm meant to create next?"

Fear shows you what to avoid.

Imagination reveals what's possible.

And in the space between those two—that's where transformation begins.

Because the power of possibility isn't reserved for visionaries.

It's available to thinkers—and you're one of them.

You've faced reality and named your fears. That awareness—painful as it can be—is your foundation.

The next question is: What now?

Once the noise clears, imagination begins. Imagination is how we design the life that fear once convinced us was impossible.

CHAPTER 5
FROM DATA TO DREAMS

Ravi excelled with data.

He could read a spreadsheet like some people read poetry, discovering patterns and predictions with mathematical precision.

Lately, however, the numbers felt... empty.

He could track engagement, conversions, and metrics, but something was missing—meaning.

One day, while building a report for a client, he realized he wasn't creating insight; he was producing output. That's when he began to ask a different question: "What do these numbers make possible?"

After one particularly quiet presentation, his manager closed the laptop and gently reiterated the question Ravi was pondering: "Ravi, your data's solid. But where's the direction? What are we building because of this?"

The question landed like a diagnosis: he wasn't leading—he was reporting.

And deep down, he knew it.

Once fear loosens its grip, imagination can finally breathe. This chapter isn't about avoiding uncertainty—it's about learning to play with it.

The Point Where Logic Stalls

Information is comforting because it promises certainty. But certainty is not the same as strategy. Data tells you what is. Design tells you what's next.

The more Ravi tried to seal every gap with additional data, the more he smothered the space where imagination breathes. He was solving yesterday's equations— beautifully—while tomorrow waited, unaddressed, just outside the slide deck.

Most people confuse accuracy with agency. Accuracy describes reality. Agency shapes it.

That's why this chapter exists. Not to talk you out of logic— but to reunite logic with imagination so you can build what doesn't exist yet.

The Meeting That Changed Everything

Two days later, Ravi sat in a cross-functional brainstorm. Marketing wanted direction. Product wanted priorities. Ops wanted feasibility. Everyone sought certainty.

He opened his laptop and then—stopped. He closed it slowly.

"I have the data," he said, "but I think we're asking the wrong question."

Heads tilted.

"What if the question isn't what happened, but what could we create if we combined what customers say they want with what they actually do?"

Silence. Then a spark.

He sketched three circles on a whiteboard:

- Signals (the numbers)
- Stories (what customers say)
- Surprise (what no one is expecting yet)

"In the overlap," he said, "is invention."

For the first time in months, the room leaned in.

Ravi wasn't just reporting. He was shaping.

Adobe's Leap: From Product to Possibility

When Adobe shifted from boxed software to Creative Cloud, they didn't chase a trend—they redesigned their relationship with customers.

On paper, the numbers warned them of:

- Short-term revenue turbulence
- Customer backlash
- Analyst skepticism

But they asked a better question:

"What future will unleash more creativity, more often?"

Subscriptions weren't a pricing trick; they were a possibility engine—continuous updates, collaboration, cloud workflows, and new tools that made creation easier than waiting for a yearly box.

Adobe moved from selling ownership to enabling momentum.

That's what imagination does: it shifts a business from proving value to creating it in real time.

The Engineer's Case for Creativity

I used to think creativity belonged solely to artists and branding teams. Engineering taught me precision, and entrepreneurship taught me speed. But reinvention revealed this:

Creativity is disciplined problem-solving directed at the unknown.

It's not chaos—it's order under construction. It's the mind doing what God designed it to do: think, choose, and build.

Fear and imagination draw from the same energy.

The energy is identical—it's just directed in opposite ways.

You can't eliminate fear, but you can retrain it.

Fear can't coexist with growth.

So we train it—deliberately.

The Insight Gap

We live in a time of information abundance but interpretation scarcity. Every day, more than 328 million terabytes of data are created globally—yet clarity is declining.

The future doesn't belong to those who can access the most information.

It belongs to those who can translate it.

This is what creativity researcher Teresa Amabile (Harvard) calls the Innovation Cycle:

Imagination + Analysis + Action $\rightarrow$ Insight.

Data without imagination is directionless.

Imagination without data is naive.

But when you bridge both, you transform noise into knowledge.

Framework: The Data-Dream Continuum

Mode	Mindset	Danger	Edge
Data	"What is?"	Paralysis by analysis	Awareness
Dream	"What if?"	Escapism	Possibility
Design	"What's next?"	Rigidity	Action

Ravi started using this framework weekly.

Instead of asking "What's wrong?" he began asking "What's possible here?"

And in that question, data became story again.

Imagination Sprint (Worksheet Introduction)

Take 15 minutes.

Set a timer and use pen and paper—no digital devices.

Researchers at the University of Tokyo (2021) found that students who wrote notes by hand remembered 40% more content and had richer conceptual recall than those who typed.

Why?

Because writing forces your brain to slow down—and thinking happens at the speed of slowness.

Your sprint:

- Write the challenge you're facing at the top of the page.
- Set a timer for 3 minutes and list every possible solution—even the absurd ones.
- When time's up, circle the three that spark curiosity, not just safety.
- Reflect: Why these three? What do they reveal about how I think?

This is your switch from data to design.

Do it now—here are five prompts, 3 minutes. No perfection, just honest velocity.

1. The Flip

Write one problem. Flip it.

If the problem were a solution in disguise, what would it teach you to build?

2. 10x Without Permission

If resources and approval were guaranteed, what is the 10x version of your idea? (Not 10% better—10x different.)

3. The 8-Year-Old

How would a child solve this? (Children ignore fake constraints. So should you—for five minutes.)

4. Human + Machine

If AI handles the repetitive and referenceable, what purely human role will you play? (Empathy, taste, discernment, meaning-making.)

5. The Faith Leap

If you believed God designed you to THINK boldly, what is the next courageous micro-step you'd take in the next 48 hours?

Don't edit. Don't self-censor. Output over optics. You're building range, not a résumé line.

You can find the full worksheet at thinkingedge.online— updated regularly with new prompts and thinking techniques.

Ravi's Micro-Win

Ravi ran a streamlined Sprint at his desk.

- The Flip → "Low engagement" became "permission to redesign the story."
- 10x → A living dashboard that surfaces opportunities, not just outcomes.
- The 8-Year-Old → "Make it like a game. People like games."
- Human + Machine → AI drafts weekly insights; Ravi curates the reasons why they matter.
- The Faith Leap → Ship a one-page prototype to his manager by Friday.

Friday came. He shipped. "Finally," his manager said, "this moves us."

It wasn't perfect. It was alive. Movement creates clarity; stagnation creates fear.

Field Notes: Data → Design Playbook

Use this quick conversion kit when you feel stuck in analysis.

- If you're overexplaining → ask: "What future does this enable?"
- If your deck is too neat → add a messy whiteboard page with three new options.
- If your idea feels small → run the 10x prompt and keep the wildest line.
- If a tool scares you → list three ways it can multiply your human edge.

- If stakeholders stall → shift the question from "Is it proven?" to "Where can we safely test?"

Teaser: The Expanded Imagination Sprint (Online)

Inside the book's reader hub, you'll find the Expanded Imagination Sprint™—a guided, printable (and updatable) worksheet that walks you through:

- A 3-layer Flip that reveals hidden assumptions
- A Constraint Collapse drill to find invisible options
- A Human Edge Inventory to define your irreplaceable role
- A 48-Hour Momentum Map to turn vision into steps

This lives online on purpose—so it can evolve as your world does.

(You'll scan a QR code later in the book to access it.)

Faith: The Architect of Action

Faith isn't the absence of data; it's the courage to build beyond it.

It doesn't ignore risk—it **integrates** it.

The future won't be led by people who know the most facts.

It will be led by those who **imagine** what's possible, **decide** what matters, and **design** what comes next.

Ravi learned that the spreadsheet is a **starting** line, not a finish line.

So will you.

Stop asking only, "What do I know?"

Start asking, "What can I design?"

Then take the smallest bold step—and let motion teach you the rest.

Reflection

Innovation isn't about finding new answers.

It's about asking better questions—and slowing down long enough to hear the answers when they come.

"We're drowning in data and starving for meaning."

Write it down. Don't just think it—write it.

Because clarity grows through ink, not pixels.

CHAPTER 6
VISION AS A SKILL

Vision used to sound like a gift—something a few rare leaders had.

But what if vision isn't a gift at all?

What if it's a skill—something anyone can practice, refine, and strengthen through deliberate attention?

Ravi's story picks up where Lena's left off: the spark of imagination turning into a system of vision.

Creativity isn't chaos—it's clarity under construction.

Vision is what gives imagination a direction to move toward.

The Moment of Seeing

When Ravi's boss, Samuel, was just starting out, he imagined success in pictures.

He sketched what a thriving store looked like—where products were placed, how customers flowed, and the emotions he wanted people to feel upon entering.

He didn't have sophisticated data, AI dashboards, or predictive tools.

He had a pencil and his imagination.

Years later, he would look back and realize that almost everything he had drawn eventually became reality: the displays, the customer experience, and the overall feeling.

Samuel hadn't stumbled into luck—he had been running mental simulations long before science had the language for it.

The Science of Seeing Ahead

When we talk about "vision," many people imagine it as abstract dreaming—wishful thinking or lofty goals recorded in notebooks.

But neuroscience reveals something extraordinary:

Your brain doesn't distinguish much between imagined action and real action.

When you vividly visualize an event—seeing it, hearing it, feeling it—your brain begins to rehearse that event as if it's happening in the moment. This is called **mental simulation**.

During these simulations, the same neural networks that control perception, motor movement, and emotion all activate in synchrony.

Your brain is constructing a future memory.

The Proof Is in the Physiology

Dr. Guang Yue at the Cleveland Clinic conducted a now-famous study with two groups:

- One group physically lifted weights.
- The other group only imagined lifting them—vividly, intentionally, every day.

After 12 weeks, the "mental" group increased muscle strength by 13.5%—without any physical movement.

Electromyography scans confirmed that the neural pathways controlling muscle activation had strengthened purely through mental rehearsal.

Their minds had trained their bodies.

This is not imagination as escapism.

It's imagination as engineering.

Why It Works

Visualization activates the **motor cortex**, **premotor areas**, and **anterior cingulate cortex**—regions linked to coordination, focus, and motivation.

When those neurons fire together repeatedly, they create new connections—a process known as **neuroplasticity**.

In simple terms:

"What the mind rehearses, the body remembers."

That's why elite athletes visualize every movement before competition, why concert pianists mentally rehearse passages without touching a key, and why visionary leaders use mental imagery to explore possible futures before committing to one.

The brain learns through repetition—whether those repetitions are physical or imagined.

When you picture a future clearly and repeatedly, your brain begins to treat it as a familiar environment. This familiarity breeds confidence, and confidence drives execution.

Vision as Neurological Priming

Vision, then, isn't fantasy—it's neurological priming.

When you visualize, your **reticular activating system (RAS)**—the brain's internal filter for relevance—starts surfacing opportunities that align with your focus.

That's why when you buy a red car, you suddenly notice red cars everywhere. You've trained your perception to pay attention.

When you vividly imagine your goals, your mind begins scanning reality for anything that matches.

You start noticing conversations, insights, and connections that support that vision.

You're not manifesting through magic.

You're manifesting through neural alignment.

Framework: The Vision Gap Analysis

There's always a gap between where you are and where you envision yourself. Most people close that gap by working harder.

Visionaries close it by thinking clearer.

Ask yourself:

- What does "success" actually look, feel, and sound like for me?

- What do I believe I'll have to sacrifice to achieve it—and is that belief true?
- What's one small visible step I can take today to make this vision slightly more tangible?

Productivity expert Cal Newport, in Deep Work, reminds us: clarity comes from depth, not speed.

Vision requires profound thought—not bursts of activity.

You can't build a future you haven't paused to envision.

The Practice: Vision Calibration

Take 15 minutes.

Grab a notebook—yes, paper and pen.

Draw two columns:

- On the left, outline your current world—your routines, responsibilities, and rhythms.
- On the right, depict your desired future—with symbols, colors, or words.

Now connect them with lines showing the gaps between what is and what could be. Label each gap: habit, mindset, relationship, resource.

Then, for each gap, ask:

- What new thinking would help me bridge this?

- What old belief would I need to release?

Don't rush this process.

And don't type it.

Writing by hand is profoundly important.

The Hidden Power of Handwriting

As mentioned earlier, handwriting activates deeper cognitive encoding—a reminder that thought becomes more intentional when ink meets paper.

In 2014, researchers Pam Mueller and Daniel Oppenheimer (UCLA) found that students who took handwritten notes understood the material far better than those who typed.

Why?

Typing allows for faster recording of information—but it bypasses comprehension.

Writing necessitates summarization and selection—slowing your brain just enough to THINK.

Neuroscientist Stanislas Dehaene refers to this as motor cognition—the connection between motion, memory, and meaning.

When you write, you encode experience into identity.

Typing captures words.

Writing captures thought.

So as you engage in your Vision Calibration exercise, use a pen.

Feel the ink flow.

Notice how slowing down sharpens your vision.

Your brain needs your hand to help it believe.

Reflection: The Architecture of Attention

Vision isn't about predicting the future—it's about preparing your mind to meet it.

The clearer your imagination of where you're going, the more your nervous system begins to align with that direction.

Athletes call this flow.

Scientists refer to it as cognitive priming.

Leaders describe it as clarity.

It's all the same truth:

Your mind is designed to create coherence between what you see internally and what you experience externally.

So don't just dream.

Rehearse.

Draw.

Write.

Think deliberately about what's next.

Because what you see with intention, you eventually create.

And what you write down, you begin to live.

Closing Thought

Vision isn't a gift reserved for the lucky.

It's a discipline available to the willing.

When you slow your mind, imagine deeply, and write what you see—you're not escaping reality.

You're authoring it.

"The future doesn't belong to those who predict it.

It belongs to those who prepare their minds to see it first."

Vision gives us direction, but awareness gives it integrity.

Before we run faster with machines, we must remember what it means to think as humans.

Chapter 7 poses the most important question of all: What can you do that AI can't?

PART III

I: IDENTIFY YOUR HUMAN EDGE—FIND WHAT MAKES YOU IRREPLACEABLE

CHAPTER 7
WHAT AI CAN'T DO

The world is obsessed with what machines can do.

Here's a question that rarely gets asked loudly enough:

"What can I do that a machine can't—consistently, courageously, and on purpose?"

In our rush to keep up, we risk forgetting the one thing that cannot be automated: conscious, value-anchored thought.

AI can simulate intelligence.

It can't generate **meaning**.

It can analyze context.

It can't **care**.

Maya: Running Faster, Feeling Less

Maya was a senior project manager who lived by dashboards—velocity charts, burndown graphs, message pings. Efficiency was her main metric, and she hit it—until she noticed something was off. The more tasks she completed, the less she felt present.

One late night, half-joking, she typed into a chatbot:

"Why do I feel like I'm running faster but going nowhere?"

It replied with tidy phrases about "cognitive load" and "burnout indicators." Useful terms. Cold comfort.

Maya stared at the screen. "You don't know what this feels like," she whispered.

That gap—between knowledge and knowing, output and ownership—is where her value resides. It's where yours does too.

Modern cognitive science refers to this as cognitive overload—when our brains process more inputs than they can organize into meaning.

Researchers at Stanford and MIT have shown that chronic multitasking lowers empathy and shortens our attention span.

Maya wasn't weak or unmotivated; her circuitry was simply saturated.

Machines handle data by design. Humans make sense of it by pausing. That's our advantage.

The Human Edge (Defined)

You don't compete with AI by working harder.

You compete by **thinking deeper**.

Your advantage is the composite of distinctly human capacities:

- **Empathy**—sensing what isn't said and choosing to honor it.
- **Discernment**—separating signal from noise when both seem convincing.
- **Taste**—a felt sense of quality, coherence, and fit.
- **Moral Imagination**—asking not only "Can we?" but "Should we?" and "What for?"
- **Faith**—acting with courage before certainty arrives.

AI can echo these qualities in tone.

Only you can embody them with integrity.

Neuroscientists describe this through mirror neurons— machines can imitate expression, but they don't experience resonance.

The Agency's Confession

When I first integrated AI into my agency, I was stunned. It could draft ad copy, spin concepts, outline strategies, and analyze performance—**in minutes**. What took hours now took seconds.

At first, it felt liberating.

Then it felt erosive.

As the **work** sped up, the **thinking** slowed down.

The more I produced, the less I recognized my voice. Clients hire me for my lens, my judgment, my way of connecting dots. Suddenly, I was generating content that was technically correct—but spiritually hollow.

I caught myself thinking:

"If I'm not careful, this tool will make me lazy in the one area I can't afford to be—my mind."

The wake-up: **I can create great content with AI—but if I don't guard my thought, my taste, and my integrity, I'll lose the very thing clients come to me for.**

So I drew a line:

AI can **accelerate** my process.

It cannot **author** my perspective.

Devil's Advocate: "But AI Will Learn Empathy, Taste, Even Strategy... Right?"

Let's entertain the strongest counterpoints—and answer them honestly.

Counter 1: "AI already writes like humans. Soon it'll 'feel' like us, too." AI can model emotional language patterns, but it cannot experience emotion. This distinction is crucial in leadership, conflict, ethics, and trust. People don't just want words that sound caring; they need decisions made by someone who is genuinely caring and accountable.

Counter 2: "Data-driven systems outperform human judgment." In stable environments with clear objectives, often yes. However, in ambiguous areas—such as brand, culture, meaning, and ethics—overreliance on past data creates blind spots. Breakthroughs arise from contrarian insight and moral courage, both of which require human risk.

Counter 3: "Speed beats soul in the market." Speed captures attention, while soul sustains loyalty. Velocity without vision erodes trust and undermines teams. Leaders who endure will combine speed with stewardship.

Counter 4: "If AI can draft the idea, why should I THINK deeply?" Because ownership isn't in the draft; it's in the decision. Your irreplaceability lies in how you choose, why you choose, and what you stand for (or walk away from).

Integrity Protocol: How to Use AI Without Losing Yourself

Here's the policy I follow in my own work—the one that restored my voice.

1. **Purpose First, Prompt Second.** Write your point of view in bullets before using any tools. If you can't articulate your stance, the model will deliver a generic one.

2. **Human Thesis, Machine Draft.** You own the thesis (what you believe), the stakes (why it matters), and the standard (what "good" looks like). Let AI draft around that—not instead of it.

3. **The Taste Test.** Read the output aloud. If it doesn't feel like you—cadence, conviction, courage—mark the bland parts. Rewrite them in your voice and add a line you would genuinely say.

4. **Add Story, Add Soul.** Every deliverable should include one lived detail, one earned insight, or one courageous sentence. If you can't find it, you're not done THINKing.

5. **Accountability Check.** Ask: "If this decision backfires, am I willing to own it?" If not, you're hiding behind the tool. Adjust.

6. **Final Filter.** Does this align with my values? Does it serve the person on the other side? If yes → ship. If no → revise.

Tools should extend your imagination; they must never replace your awareness.

This discipline isn't merely philosophical—it's neurological.

The prefrontal cortex, responsible for judgment and long-term reasoning, activates most when we slow down and consciously decide.

Every time you pause before accepting an AI suggestion, you're not wasting time—you're strengthening the part of your brain that protects integrity.

Patagonia's Principle: Numbers Don't Carry Meaning—People Do

When Patagonia decided to give away its profits to protect the planet, spreadsheets didn't drive that choice. Conviction did. The data could describe impact, but it couldn't define identity. Purpose provided their intelligence with direction—and customers trusted them for it.

That's the key:

Numbers can optimize a business.

Only meaning can **orient** it.

Practice: Slow Thinking in a Fast World

To sharpen your human edge, train your capacity for intentional thought:

Pause → Name → Ask → Align → Act.

- **Pause:** 60 seconds of stillness before big decisions.
- **Name:** What emotion is in the room (mine/theirs)?
- **Ask:** What's the real question beneath the request?
- **Align:** Does this align with my values and long-term vision?
- **Act:** Choose the smallest courageous step—and own it.

Five minutes of thought outperforms five hours of noise.

Psychologist Daniel Kahneman described this as the shift from "System 1" to "System 2"—moving from reflex to reflection.

The goal isn't to slow down for its own sake; it's to regain awareness before automation.

The Co-Creation Map: Who Does What—You vs. AI

When in doubt, use this quick allocation:

Stage	Human Leads	AI Assists
Sense (listen, empathize)	Interviews, nuance, reading the room	Summaries, sentiment clustering
Define (choose the problem)	Priorities, ethics, tradeoffs	Organizing inputs

Stage	Human Leads	AI Assists
Imagine (explore options)	"What if," taste, bold leaps	Generating variations
Decide (pick a path)	Stakes, responsibility, values	Risk/impact scaffolding
Build (ship, iterate)	Quality control, voice, ownership	Drafts, checklists, QA passes

Your non-negotiable: **You** make the call. Every time.

The Erosion I Refused (Your Anecdote, Fully Developed)

There was a month when my agency's output soared. Proposals polished. Captions snappy. Reports immaculate. The pipeline looked healthy.

But in client calls, I heard it:"Annabelen, this is good... but it doesn't sound like you."

They were right. I had optimized for speed and sacrificed **signature**. I could produce more—but I was delivering less of me.

So I rebuilt the process:

- **My Thought First:** I start with a one-paragraph thesis in my words—what I believe and why it matters here.
- **AI Second:** I let the model draft options from that thesis.

- **Voice Pass:** I add the line only I would say—the uncomfortable truth, the lived detail, the precise metaphor.
- **Integrity Check:** If I wouldn't defend it in front of a room, it doesn't leave my desk.

Output remained fast. My voice returned. Clients noticed. They weren't paying for speed; they were investing in **judgment.**

Faith in the Age of Algorithms

Faith is the counter-algorithm.

It is the discipline of holding a thought aligned with truth when metrics waver and trends shout.

Faith doesn't deny data. It directs it.

Faith chooses meaning over momentum, stewardship over spectacle, long-term over likes.

In the decade ahead, the world will drown in information. The ones who rise will be those who still THINK for themselves, pairing tools with conscience, speed with soul.

Reflection: Protect Your Edge (Today)

- Where have I traded convenience for consciousness?
- Which deliverables need a Voice Pass before they ship?
- What one decision this week deserves slow thinking?

- If my name stands behind this, what would I change?

Your edge isn't found in output.

It's found in **awareness**—and in the courage to keep your mind awake while the world automates.

AI will evolve.

You are designed to transform.

Begin with a thought you're willing to own—because that's the one thing no algorithm can ever automate: the human act of awareness.

CHAPTER 8
THE EDGE EFFECT

In ecology, the edge effect describes what happens where two ecosystems meet—forest and meadow, river and ocean, city and sky.

At the edges, life multiplies.

Species interact.

Diversity flourishes.

Unique growth occurs that can't survive elsewhere.

It's not always comfortable—storms form there, too—but the tension between two environments gives rise to transformation.

That's where we find ourselves today—at the intersection of human intelligence and artificial intelligence.

Not replacement.

Not rivalry.

Integration.

The future belongs to those who learn to live, think, and create at this junction—where logic meets empathy, data meets discernment, and speed meets soul.

That's where leverage resides.

Where the Edges Meet

When AI first entered Ravi's workflow, he approached it cautiously.

After years of leading a small nonprofit team, he relied on human relationships, conversation, and community trust for decision-making.

Now, suddenly, a dashboard promised insights from thousands of data points—survey responses, feedback logs, social sentiment.

He admired the precision but felt uneasy. The numbers spoke clearly, yet something was missing.

So one afternoon, instead of running another analysis, Ravi closed the dashboard and invited his team into the conference room. He printed a handful of responses and asked everyone to read one aloud.

By the third story, the room fell silent.

One respondent—a mother of two—had shared her feelings of invisibility in the system they were trying to improve. The AI's sentiment score marked her as "neutral."

Ravi could see she was anything but neutral. She was tired.

He leaned back and said quietly, "The numbers told me what people said.

These stories reveal what they meant."

In that moment, Ravi shifted from using AI as an oracle to employing it as an instrument. A lens, not a leader.

A partner, not a prophet.

That was his edge moment—the point where data met humanity and something deeper emerged.

The Ecology of Innovation

Every edge—ecological or technological—follows the same pattern:

1. Diversity fuels adaptation.

When different systems overlap, resilience increases. Collaboration between humans and technology opens new pathways for creativity.

2. Boundaries breed invention.

Innovation often begins where friction exists. Growth requires a balance between comfort and curiosity.

3. Balance sustains progress.

Excessive control stifles diversity; too little direction leads to chaos. The sweet spot—purposeful integration—is where innovation thrives.

The same holds true for this new era. AI is fast, precise, and vast.

Humans are intuitive, ethical, and aware.

The most powerful ideas will emerge from the overlap— from individuals who learn to think at the edge of both.

The Edge Equation: Human + Machine $\longrightarrow$ Multiplication

AI doesn't multiply **worth**; it multiplies intention.

Feed it clarity, empathy, and curiosity, and it scales those.

Feed it bias, ego, or haste, and it scales those too.

That's why awareness—not automation—is your true productivity multiplier.

"AI is not your rival; it's your reflection."

It reveals the quality of your input—the integrity of your thought.

Machines perform.

Humans perceive.

And when you merge those capacities with care, you create outcomes that neither could achieve alone.

Example: Apple's Edge Advantage

When Steve Jobs returned to Apple in 1997, the company had advanced technology but lacked soul.

He didn't rebuild it through faster processors; he revitalized it through design thinking—a practice of merging human empathy with technical feasibility.

Design thinking poses three questions relevant to every AI decision today:

- What's desirable for people?
- What's feasible for technology?
- What's viable for the mission or business?

True innovation occurs at the intersection of human desire and machine capability. The iPhone wasn't created through algorithms; it emerged from awareness.

This principle applies to your work as well:

AI provides tools; you provide taste.

AI offers data; you provide direction.

AI delivers speed; you provide sense.

Framework: The Edge Map

Use this map to identify your zones of leverage—areas where your unique human strengths align with your tools:

AREA	HUMAN STRENGTH	AI'S ROLE	TOGETHER THEY CREATE...
Strategy	Judgment, ethics, narrative thinking	Pattern recognition	Clarity and conviction
Creativity	Vision, metaphor, emotional intelligence	Ideation speed	New possibilities
Communication	Empathy, storytelling, persuasion	Drafting, summarizing	Authentic amplification
Decision-Making	Discernment, long-term view	Data synthesis	Informed intuition
Learning	Curiosity, adaptability	Personalized insight	Continuous growth

Circle your top two "edge zones."

Ask: Where does my humanity enhance technology's effectiveness? Then spend 80% of your time there.

Because innovation doesn't happen in extremes—it thrives in overlaps.

Ravi's Turning Point

Months later, Ravi's project reports transformed.

They still featured data visualizations and metrics, but now began with human stories.

Each presentation opened with a single voice—a parent, a teacher, a volunteer—before revealing the patterns beneath their words.

His board noticed a change: engagement soared.

The insights felt personal. Authentic.

They inspired action.

One colleague remarked, "It's like you brought the soul back to the spreadsheet."

Ravi smiled.

He hadn't rejected AI; he had refined it.

That's the essence of working at the edge—using tools to amplify truth, not replace it.

Exercise: Your Edge Audit

Take ten quiet minutes—ideally with a pen, not a keyboard.

- What do I do best that no machine can replicate?
- Where could AI extend my impact without diluting my judgment?
- What task have I been resisting due to fear of being "replaced"?
- How could I approach it instead as a collaboration?

As you write, remember: handwriting slows thought enough to notice nuance.

It turns reflection into revelation.

You're not just listing skills—you're locating your edge ecosystem.

Closing Reflection

The edge is not a place of fear; it's a space for growth.

It's where your limits meet your potential—and where new life begins to flourish.

When you stand there consciously, with curiosity and humility, you don't just survive disruption.

You shape it.

Because the real power of AI lies not in what it does.

It's in who you become when you learn to use it effectively.

"The future won't be written by code alone. It will be authored by those who think at the edge—where humanity and technology meet with meaning."

CHAPTER 9
FAITH, CHOICE & CALLING

Most people THINK courage feels like bravery—chest out, head high, no fear.

That's a lie.

Courage is trembling hands that click "submit" anyway.

It's the late-night decision to stay in the game even when confidence is waning.

It's showing up curious when you'd rather hide.

Courage isn't the absence of fear.

It's the refusal to be ruled by it.

And that's the secret to evolving—you don't wait to feel ready.

You move, and readiness meets you on the way. The email subject line read: **"Leadership Review."**

Ravi froze.

He knew it was coming—the quarterly check-in with his manager and the director of strategy. Still, his stomach tightened. His heart quickened. His fingers hovered over the mouse.

He'd done good work—great work, even.

The nonprofit campaign had gone viral. The team was energized. The client was thrilled.

But lately, he'd sensed a quiet shift in the office—a subtle undercurrent of uncertainty. AI had started taking on more analytical tasks. His data reports were auto-generated. Dashboards maintained themselves.

He was still essential.

But for how long?

The Moment Between Control and Surrender

He opened the email.

Meeting at 2:00 p.m. "We'll review recent outcomes and next steps. We'll also discuss future team composition."

Future team composition.

He knew what it meant: roles were being reevaluated.

The familiar voice crept in—not facts, but fears.

What if I'm next? What if all this adapting isn't enough?

He reached for his leather notebook—the one for reflection, not reports—and wrote three words:

Faith. Choice. Calling.

Not answers. Anchors.

The Meeting

At 2:00, Ravi stepped into the glass conference room. Mark, his manager, nodded.

"Your work this quarter has been outstanding," Mark said. "The Why Map campaign—brilliant. The client feedback has been incredible."

Relief flickered. Then came the next line.

"We're also restructuring. We're investing heavily in AI systems for analytics, forecasting, and reporting. We'll be shifting human roles toward strategy and leadership—fewer analysts, more decision-makers."

The words blurred for a moment—the way they do when your mind is deciding if this is a threat or an invitation.

A voice inside whispered, They're replacing what you do.

Another, steadier voice replied, They're inviting you to evolve.

Ravi chose which one to feed.

"I've been thinking about that," he said. "What if we use AI not just for analysis, but for storytelling—translating our findings into real human outcomes?"

Mark looked up. "Go on."

As Ravi spoke, he felt the room shift—from evaluation to collaboration.

He wasn't being reviewed. He was being **reframed**.

When the Ground Shifts (Again)

Afterward, Ravi sat in his car, hands on the wheel, not ready to drive. Coffee in the air. AC humming. The world moved forward whether or not he did.

He remembered the first time he felt this—years earlier, when automation replaced half his team's data-cleaning tasks. He'd adapted then.

Now it was happening again—bigger, faster, closer to who he thought he was.

What if I'm just chasing relevance that keeps running ahead of me?

It wasn't just professional. It was personal.

He wasn't just scared of losing a job; he was scared of losing his identity.

The Truth About Evolution

Evolution isn't about becoming someone new; it's about becoming **more deeply you.**

It's not about abandoning the past but integrating it—letting experience fuel you instead of instilling fear.

Every time life asks you to evolve, it tests one thing:

Can you remain faithful to your purpose while allowing your form to change?

That's courage: not knowing the outcome—and moving forward anyway.

Mark's Call

That night, Mark called. "You okay?"

"Yeah," Ravi replied. "Just... processing."

"I've been there," Mark chuckled. "Every time the world changes, people think it's the end. It's not the end; it's the next beginning.

"Remember my retail story? We'd rearrange the store every quarter—not to confuse people, but to make them see it again. Familiarity numbs awareness, while change awakens it.

"Maybe that's what's happening to you. You're being rearranged so you can view yourself differently. Evolution isn't loss; it's awareness expanding."

Ravi listened as panic eased into perspective.

Choice: The Architecture of Agency

Every disruption demands a decision.

Every decision defines who you are.

Ravi asked a sharper question:

"If AI can handle tasks, what human value becomes even more vital?"

The answer came quickly—empathy, storytelling, stewardship.

These were the very elements that made his work human-first.

He couldn't control the organization's evolution, but he could control his response to it.

He chose to be irreplaceable—not by resisting technology, but by redefining what it means to lead.

He would be the voice translating numbers into narratives, data into decisions, reports into **relationships.**

That's what choice looks like when fear is loud but purpose is louder.

Calling: The Invitation Within

Calling isn't always dramatic; it's often a persistent question:

"What am I meant to make possible here?"

His worth wasn't tied to a title; it was tied to his contribution.

The mission hadn't changed—the method had.

Maybe his calling wasn't to continue what he'd always done, but to guide others through the same uncertainty he once feared.

The anxiety didn't vanish; now it had purpose.

Faith without movement is fantasy.

Choice without calling is noise.

When all three align, clarity emerges.

Framework: The Inner Alignment Model

Element	Definition	Question to Ask
Faith	Holding a direction without evidence	What truth do I trust even when I can't see the outcome?

Element	Definition	Question to Ask
Choice	Acting in alignment with that truth	What's one action that reflects who I want to be?
Calling	Where that truth meets a need	Where is my contribution needed most right now?

When the world feels unstable, this model restores orientation.

Faith grounds you. Choice propels you. Calling sustains you.

The Fear → Forward Framework

Transforming Anxiety into Aligned Action

Fear is not weakness; it's a signal—it appears at the boundary between who you are and who you're becoming. The key isn't to silence it; it's to translate it before it becomes your ceiling.

1. Name It with Honesty (not judgment).

Generalities hide fear. Precision shrinks it.

Write exactly what you hear in your head:

I'm afraid I won't be relevant. I'm afraid people will outgrow me. I'm afraid I'll lose what I've built.

2. Interrogate with Compassion.

Ask: Is this fear protecting me or preventing me?

Notice where you feel it (chest, gut, jaw). Breathe into that place. You're not deleting fear—you're making space for wisdom to speak louder.

3. Translate into Direction.

Ask: What is this fear asking me to pay attention to? If it had a message, what would it be?

Then convert it into movement: learn, speak up, delegate, collaborate.

4. Take One Visible Step.

Not a leap—a proof point. Send the email. Ask the question. Draft the idea. Try the tool.

Evidence teaches your nervous system: We can do hard things and still be safe.

5. Reflect with Faith.

Ask: What is this experience teaching me about who I'm becoming?

(If it aligns with your worldview, also ask: What might God be strengthening in me through this discomfort?)

Faith reframes fear from threat to teacher.

Every time you move through fear instead of away from it, you retrain your system to see change as development, not danger.

Fear's language is "Stop." Faith's language is "Step."

Courage Is Not Confidence

Most people think courage feels like confidence—chest out, chin up, fear gone.

That's a myth.

Courage is trembling hands that click "submit" anyway.

It's showing up curious when you'd rather hide.

It doesn't cancel fear; it carries it forward.

Readiness doesn't precede action.

It meets you after you move.

Ravi didn't leave that week with a new title.

He left with a new posture.

Faith gave him focus.

Choice gave him movement.

Calling gave him meaning.

Together, they gave him peace.

Faith: The Engine of Evolution

Faith isn't blind optimism. It's anchored trust.

The decision to believe that even unchosen change can refine what comfort never could.

Faith says, You're not being replaced; you're being redirected. Faith says, You haven't fallen behind; you're being prepared for what's ahead.

That's the essence of courage—not moving because you're fearless, but moving because you're faithful.

Reflect with Faith

Faith reframes fear from threat to teacher.

Ask:

"What is this experience trying to teach me about who I'm becoming?" "What might God be strengthening in me through this discomfort?"

Faith doesn't promise no fear—it promises purpose within it.

When you reflect through faith, you turn anxiety into awareness and movement into meaning.

Final Thought

Every time you move through fear instead of away from it, you retrain your entire system—body, mind, and spirit—to see change not as danger, but as divine development.

Fear's language is "Stop."

Faith's language is "Step."

And every time you choose to step, you're proving to yourself that the evolution you feared is the transformation you were made for.

Reflection: The Next You

- Where are you clinging to an old version of yourself that no longer fits?
- What fear are you mistaking for failure—when it's growth in disguise?
- What single decision this week would align you more with who you're becoming than who you've been?

Write it. Say it aloud.

Then take one deliberate step.

Courage doesn't come from knowing you'll succeed.

It comes from understanding that you're evolving.

Every evolution begins with one thought: **I'm willing to keep becoming.**

PART IV

N: NAVIGATE THE NOISE — DISCERN AND DECIDE WISELY

CHAPTER 10
OVERWHELMED BY EVERYTHING

"You learned earlier that stillness isn't silence—it's signal.

Back then, it sparked your creativity.

Now, it helps you survive the noise."

The noise never truly stops.

Notifications, updates, headlines, chatter—each tugging at your attention like static on a signal.

We live in an age where speed is celebrated and stillness is suspect.

We measure how quickly we respond, not how wisely we decide.

Midnight, Again

It was nearly midnight when Maya looked up and realized two hours had vanished.

The glow of her phone was the only light in the room—a cold, steady pulse against her skin. Her thumb moved almost by muscle memory. Tap. Scroll. Refresh.

She told herself she was "staying informed.

"That this was research—part of her work, part of keeping up.

She called it research to quiet the guilt—but deep down, she knew she wasn't gathering insight; she was escaping responsibility. The scrolling gave her the illusion of productivity while her true purpose lay untouched.

And deep down, she realized: she wasn't working anymore. She was wandering.

It had started innocently enough—an article about AI ethics, something she genuinely cared about.

Then a tweet thread on marketing trends.

Then a video about productivity hacks.

Then another about the best morning routines of successful people.

Before she knew it, she was watching an apartment tour in Seoul, analyzing the color palette of someone else's living room while her own thoughts lingered in the dark, waiting to be heard.

She wasn't learning. She was looping.

Her eyes were open, but her mind had gone quiet—a blur of borrowed opinions and endless information.

Each scroll offered a flicker of stimulation, the illusion of progress. But nothing stuck. Nothing formed.

Her brain felt full yet hollow—like eating sugar for dinner.

And in that strange, suspended moment between clicks, she finally heard her own thought whisper through the noise:

"Why do I feel more tired the more I know?"

She set the phone down, face down, and stared at the ceiling.

Her pulse raced, as if her body was running while her purpose lagged behind.

That's when it hit her.

This wasn't curiosity anymore.

It was drift—the kind that feels productive because it mimics motion.

She wasn't exploring the world.

She was escaping herself.

The Age of Infinite Input

This is the quiet crisis of our time: we are drowning in information and starving for wisdom.

We know more than ever—and understand less.

We connect more—and feel lonelier.

We consume constantly—but rarely digest.

Information is supposed to empower us. Instead, it exhausts us.

The truth? **Our minds were never designed for infinity.**

The average person now processes more data in a single day than someone in the 15th century would in a lifetime. Notifications, updates, podcasts, messages, analytics, articles—all compete for the same limited attention span.

We've mistaken awareness for effectiveness. We THINK staying "in the know" equals staying in control. But the opposite occurs: the more we consume, the less we create.

Because when everything feels urgent, nothing feels important.

Yahoo!: The Company That Knew Too Much

In the early 2000s, Yahoo! dominated the internet. It offered email, news, search, finance, music, and even a dating site. It acquired over 100 companies, chasing every promising opportunity.

But with each acquisition came increased complexity, noise, and distractions.

While Yahoo! attempted to be everything, Google quietly focused on one thing: search.

By trying to know everything, Yahoo! forgot its purpose. It collapsed under the weight of its own information.

That's what happens to people, too.

We collect, scroll, bookmark, subscribe—and in the process, we lose the clarity that provides direction.

Knowledge without focus isn't power; it's paralysis.

Information Is Not Wisdom

Once, scarcity was the enemy.

We fought for access to books, mentors, and ideas.

Now abundance has become the new scarcity.

Knowledge is everywhere, but attention has become priceless.

We are flooded with opinions yet starving for orientation.

Drowning in data, we thirst for discernment.

We confuse being connected with being conscious.

That's what Maya was feeling—the invisible fatigue of an overfed, undernourished mind.

When Attention Becomes a Commodity

If you've ever wondered why it's so hard to stop scrolling, remember:

You're not the customer—you're the product.

Every ping, swipe, and algorithmic nudge is engineered to hijack your attention and resell it.

Each For You page is really For Profit.

The system doesn't reward thought; it rewards reaction.

And the longer you drift in that cycle, the farther you travel from yourself.

Be Still and Know

Scripture doesn't say, "Be busy and know that I am God."

It says, "Be still."

Stillness isn't passivity; it's leadership of the mind.

When you pause, you reclaim your filter.

You choose what deserves your attention instead of letting algorithms decide for you.

In stillness, you remember who's driving.

The Drift Disguised as Discipline

Maya told herself she was "researching trends."

In reality, she was rehearsing anxiety.

Every link promised progress but delivered paralysis.

Every new insight blurred into static.

She had built a routine of reaction—always catching up, never catching her breath.

That's what drifting looks like now: busyness without breakthrough.

The Noise Detox (24 Hours That Could Change Your Brain)

To test your relationship with input, try this:

For one day, perform a Noise Detox—not as punishment, but as practice.

1. Mute the Machine.

Turn off notifications, badges, and alerts. Let the world wait for you.

2. Start Your Morning in Silence.

No podcasts, no emails, no scrolling.

Spend ten minutes with a pen and a blank page instead.

Write what's on your mind, unfiltered. Let your thoughts hear themselves.

3. Use Your Hands.

Cook, walk, doodle, garden—anything analog.

Research from the University of Tokyo (2021) found that handwriting and tactile motion enhance retention and reduce neural noise.

Writing slows your mind to the speed of thought—and that's where insight catches up.

4. End with Reflection, Not Consumption.

Before bed, ask:

- What ideas lingered with me today?
- What truly mattered once the noise subsided?

Write them by hand. Typing invites speed; writing invites honesty.

Clarity resides beneath the digital dust.

From Data to Discernment

The goal isn't to escape technology—it's to govern it.

Discernment isn't about rejecting information; it's about filtering it through purpose.

Without that filter, we react to everything and reflect on nothing.

That's why wisdom feels so rare.

In a world of acceleration, discernment requires slowness.

You can't hear your own calling if you're constantly echoing someone else's content.

Reflection Exercise: The Input Audit

Grab your notebook—yes, the paper one.

- List the five inputs you consume most (feeds, shows, mentors, podcasts).
- Next to each, note how you feel afterward—energized or anxious? Expanded or diminished?
- Circle the one you'll reduce this week. Replace it with five minutes of stillness.

That's where your original ideas reside—the ones no algorithm can supply.

When you quiet the noise, a different kind of signal emerges—not louder, but truer.

The next step is to establish a repeatable method to test that signal, separating truth from trend and wisdom from noise.

That's where we go next.

CHAPTER 11
THE DISCERNMENT SYSTEM

Lena stared at her laptop screen, the headline glowing like a warning flare:

"AI Experts Predict 70% of Jobs Gone by 2030."

Her stomach clenched.

She'd seen versions of this article countless times—each slightly different, each triggering the same cycle of worry, research, and what-if spirals.

Was it true?

Was it exaggerated?

Was it even written by a human?

She copied the headline into a search bar and found six more articles quoting each other, none linking back to the original study.

It was noise—well-packaged, well-intentioned, but still noise.

That's when it hit her:

She didn't just need to consume less. She needed to discern more.

The Age of Credibility Confusion

In the early 2000s, as digital news exploded, the New York Times faced a similar problem: information overload.

Blogs, influencers, and digital tabloids were producing content faster than truth could catch up.

People stopped trusting news not because they didn't need it, but because they couldn't tell whom to believe.

The Times had a choice: chase clicks or rebuild credibility.

They chose the harder path.

They shifted from ad-based revenue (measured by volume) to a subscription model (measured by trust).

It was a bet on discernment—believing people would pay not for more content, but for verified, contextual, thoughtful journalism.

And it worked. Because in an age of noise, credibility became currency.

We live in an era where information is instant but interpretation is scarce.

Anyone can publish. Anyone can comment.

Authority now shares the same font as opinion.

That's not cynicism—it's context.

Once, institutions filtered information for us—editors, peer reviewers, teachers.

Now, each of us is our own editor-in-chief.

This shift makes discernment—the ability to evaluate truth amid abundance—the defining skill of this century.

That's where your personal discernment begins.

The Discernment System: 4 Steps to Thinking Clearly

Discernment is not instinct; it's a process.

It allows thinkers to separate the credible from the convincing and the useful from the urgent.

Discernment isn't merely skepticism; it's stewardship—of your attention, trust, and choices.

Here's the framework—a system that helps you think clearly even when information feels overwhelming.

It's a **repeatable thought process** that protects you from drifting, manipulation, and reactionary decisions.

Credibility → Context → Contradiction → Conclusion

Let's unpack each step.

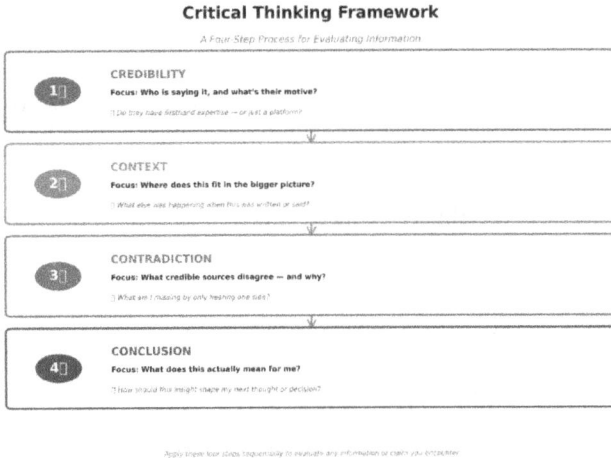

Critical Thinking Framework

A Four-Step Process for Evaluating Information

1. **CREDIBILITY**
Focus: Who is saying it, and what's their motive?
Do they have firsthand expertise — or just a platform?

2. **CONTEXT**
Focus: Where does this fit in the bigger picture?
What else was happening when this was written or said?

3. **CONTRADICTION**
Focus: What credible sources disagree — and why?
What am I missing by only hearing one side?

4. **CONCLUSION**
Focus: What does this actually mean for me?
How should this insight shape my next thought or decision?

Apply these four steps sequentially to evaluate any information or claim you encounter.

1. Credibility—Who's Speaking and Why It Matters

The internet has given everyone a microphone, but not all voices deserve your attention. Influence is not synonymous with integrity.

Followers are not equivalent to facts.

Before internalizing a claim, pause and ask:

- Who is this person?
- What do they gain if I believe them?
- Have they demonstrated experience or merely enthusiasm?

Credibility doesn't always stem from credentials; it can also reflect consistency—people who've lived what they teach over time.

In the age of AI-written content, source integrity becomes your superpower.

Pro tip: If you can't trace an idea to a person who has experienced its consequences, don't let it shape your beliefs.

2. Context—Where Does This Fit in the Bigger Picture?

Information without context is distortion.

A quote, statistic, or viral claim can be technically true yet contextually misleading.

For example, you may have seen "AI will replace 70% of jobs."

However, the original study might actually state: "70% of jobs will change in function due to automation."

This distinction is crucial.

Context reveals the difference between fear and foresight.

Always ask:

– What's the timeline here?
– What's the scope?

– What variables are being left out?

A single statistic is never the complete story; it's merely a sentence in a paragraph you haven't finished reading.

AI systems excel at providing content, but they often lack context. They can present every statistic but not the narrative those numbers inhabit.

That's your role—the human interpreter.

Discernment means considering information within its environment, not in isolation.

Context transforms data into wisdom.

3. Contradiction—What Do Credible Sources Disagree About and Why?

We are taught to seek agreement, but growth arises from disagreement.

Contradiction isn't confusion; it's calibration.

It sharpens our thinking.

When two views clash, it doesn't necessarily mean one is wrong; it indicates you've reached the boundary of understanding.

Ask:

- What's the opposing view, and what truth might it contain?
- What would someone who disagrees say, and could they be partly right?
- Am I reacting to this information because it challenges my comfort, or because it violates my conscience?

Contradiction broadens perspective.

It fosters humility—the willingness to see from another angle.

Without contradiction, you risk ending up in **intellectual echo chambers**—believing you're informed while remaining insulated.

True thinkers don't fear being wrong; they fear being closed.

Contradiction is not confusion—it's calibration.

Smart thinkers actively seek friction because truth reveals itself in contrast.

If everyone in your feed agrees, your perspective isn't expanding; it's echoing.

Lena practiced this: for every article predicting doom, she found one forecasting opportunity.

The tension between them didn't paralyze her; it clarified her thinking.

Contradiction helps you refine, not retreat.

Pro tip: Don't avoid opinions that challenge yours. Invite them to sharpen you—like grit that polishes an edge.

4. Conclusion—What Does This Actually Mean for Me?

Conclusion doesn't mean you've "figured it out."

It means you've **synthesized** enough information to act with integrity and awareness.

Ask yourself:

- What did I learn that truly matters here?
- What am I certain enough about to act on?
- What will I continue to explore—without rushing to certainty?

Good conclusions are open-ended. They're confident enough to move forward and humble enough to keep listening.

And the highest form of conclusion is action.

Discernment that doesn't translate into decision is just mental clutter.

As you refine your discernment system, remember this truth:

Wisdom isn't what you know. It's how you use what you trust.

Information alone won't save you.

Interpretation will.

The goal of discernment isn't to collect facts. It's to extract meaning.

To ask, "What does this actually require of me?"

Lena realized she didn't need to predict AI's future—she needed to decide how to stay adaptable within it.

That's the purpose of discernment: to translate data into direction.

Knowing is gathering the dots.

Thinking is connecting them.

Wisdom is choosing what to do once the picture appears.

How Lena Applied the Discernment System

The next morning, Lena tried something new.

Instead of opening ten tabs, she opened one.

She read the article slowly, asking herself each step of the framework:

- Credibility: Who's behind this piece—and what's their goal?
- Context: What's the larger story this data lives in?
- Contradiction: Who would disagree—and why might they have a point?
- Conclusion: What's my next step based on what I've learned?

By the end, she had one page of notes—not twenty tabs of noise.

For the first time in weeks, her mind felt still enough to THINK again.

Practice: The 10-Minute Thought Audit

Once a week, take ten minutes—no screens—and write by hand:

- What idea or claim impacted me this week?
- Who said it—and why do I trust them?
- What context might I be missing?
- Who sees this differently—and what can I learn from them?
- What does this mean for my next decision?

Writing forces ownership.

Typing invites reaction; handwriting invites reflection.

It slows your thinking to its natural rhythm—the pace of wisdom.

When to Trust Your Gut

Data can guide decisions, but intuition filters them.

Your gut is not magic—it's accumulated pattern recognition.

If something sounds true but feels off, pause.

If something feels true but sounds implausible, research.

Trust isn't binary. It's built in layers—evidence, alignment, intuition.

True discernment respects all three.

Case Study: The New York Times Pivot

In 2011, The New York Times faced collapsing ad revenue and a credibility crisis.

Rather than chasing clicks, they made a radical choice: go deeper, not louder.

They introduced a subscription model based on trust—betting that readers would pay for reliable reporting.

It worked.

By 2024, the paper had over 10 million paying subscribers and became a masterclass in discernment economics: proof that people crave clarity in an age of noise.

That's your takeaway—trust is the new currency.

And discernment is how you mint it.

Reflection: Build Your Filter

At the top of a clean page, write: "I will not outsource my thinking."

Below it, create your personal discernment code—three or four lines that define how you choose what to believe:

- I will pause before reacting.
- I will seek context before conviction.
- I will invite contradiction before conclusion.
- I will act only on what aligns with my values.

That's not just a mindset; it's a manifesto.

It's how you maintain your humanity in a world driven by algorithms.

Once you learn to filter truth from noise, the next challenge arises:

How do you apply that truth?

How do you move from discernment to decision—from clarity to confident action?

That's where we go next.

CHAPTER 12

WISDOM IN THE AGE OF ABUNDANCE

The morning light spilled through the conference room windows as Samuel waited for the group to arrive.

He had been invited as an outside advisor—a consultant, yes, but not the kind armed with slides and jargon.

Samuel brought something rarer: clarity.

Maya had met him years earlier during a leadership retreat. He had spoken just once that weekend, for less than ten minutes, but those moments had resonated deeper than any keynote.

He had said,
"We used to worry about not knowing enough.

Now we worry because we know too much."

That sentence had lingered with her.

Today, the team had gathered—Lena, Ravi, Maya—each feeling a different kind of overwhelm.

The noise of abundance was wearing on them. Every decision felt urgent, every opinion valid, every piece of data demanding attention.

Samuel listened as they spoke, nodding occasionally, allowing the words to empty out until silence filled the room.

Then, finally, he asked quietly,
"What do you think wisdom looks like—here, in this age of too much?"

The Illusion of More

Ravi leaned forward first. "It feels like the more we know, the less we understand," he said.

Maya nodded. "And the less we trust our own judgment."

Samuel smiled gently.

"That's because abundance is a test," he said. "Not of access, but of alignment."

He leaned back in his chair. "Information isn't scarce anymore. But focus is. Attention is. Meaning is."

He let that sit for a moment.

"When everything feels possible," he continued, "nothing feels clear. And when everyone has data, few take responsibility for interpretation. That's what wisdom restores—the courage to interpret what you already know."

He paused, then added quietly,
"Information describes the world.

Wisdom designs your place in it."

The Wisdom Gap

Maya wrote that down as Ravi looked up.

Samuel continued, "We used to rely on scarcity for direction. Limited choices forced us to make decisions. Now, abundance overwhelms us—not because we lack access, but because we never stop accessing."

He glanced at each of them. "We're over-informed but under-guided. That's not failure; it's the condition of our age. However, you can reverse it."

The Amazon Example: The Discipline of Obsession

Samuel walked to the whiteboard and drew a small circle.

In the center, he wrote one word: Purpose.

Then, he drew a dozen arrows radiating outward.

"This," he said, "is what happens when abundance meets distraction."

He paused, then added another circle, labeled: **Amazon.**

"When Jeff Bezos founded Amazon, it could have been anything—a retail, tech, or logistics company. In truth, it became all of those. But they didn't grow by chasing opportunities; they grew by focusing on one obsession: the customer."

He turned back to the group.

"Every decision passed through that filter. Every idea had to answer one question: 'Does this make life better for the customer?' If not, it didn't matter how clever or profitable it seemed."

Samuel smiled.

"That's wisdom in motion. Focused abundance. Not less opportunity—disciplined opportunity."

From Information to Interpretation

Lena scribbled notes. "So wisdom isn't about knowing more," she said slowly. "It's about knowing how to use what you already have."

Samuel nodded. "Exactly. Information accumulates. Wisdom distills. It's not what you collect; it's what you comprehend."

He continued, "Most people live like data warehouses—full of input but empty of insight.

The wise don't hoard information; they interpret it. They ask, 'What does this mean right now?'"

He paused before adding, "That's the difference between noise and knowledge.

One fills you.

The other shapes you."

The Four Pillars of Modern Wisdom

Samuel turned back to the board and wrote four words:

Gather Lightly → Interpret Deeply → Apply Slowly → Anchor Spiritually.

He underlined each one and explained.

1. Gather Lightly

"Not every idea deserves entry," he said. "Attention is your most limited resource. Guard it."

He looked around the table. "Don't mistake staying updated for staying aware. Wisdom begins with the discipline of selective intake."

Then he smiled at Maya.

"Every yes to information is a no to reflection. Choose carefully."

2. Interpret Deeply

"When something captures your attention, stop scrolling and start studying."

He looked at Lena.

"Ask: What is this really saying? How does it align with what I already know to be true? What would happen if I acted on it?"

He let the question linger.

"This is where meaning is made. Not in consuming but in connecting."

3. Apply Slowly

"Quick thinking prompts movement," Samuel said. "Slow thinking creates momentum."

He tapped the table gently.

"Wisdom requires time to test. Fast action without reflection leads to correction.

Reflection before action leads to alignment."

Ravi nodded, quietly writing that down.

4. Anchor Spiritually

Then Samuel's tone softened.

"And finally—anchor it all in spirit. Wisdom isn't just intellect; it's integrity."

He paused. "Ask what feels true, not just what sounds true. Wisdom always includes conscience."

He looked at the team, meeting each gaze.

"You can automate knowledge, but you can't automate wisdom. Wisdom requires presence."

The Letter

Later that evening, after everyone had left, Samuel sat alone at the table and opened his journal—a habit he had maintained for years.

He began to write:

"We are surrounded by abundance—of ideas, data, and opportunity.

But the test of our time is not access; it's awareness.

Wisdom isn't about being first or fastest.

It's about being faithful—to truth, purpose, and people."

He paused, pen hovering over the page.

Then he added one final line:

"Don't chase being right.

Chase being rooted."

He closed the notebook and exhaled slowly.

The room was quiet again—the kind of quiet that invites stillness rather than demands silence.

Reflection: Practicing Wisdom

- What decision in your life needs interpretation rather than more information?
- What abundance is overwhelming you right now—options, opinions, or opportunities?
- How could you apply a single organizing question (like Amazon's "customer obsession") to your own priorities?
- Where do you need to slow down, breathe, and anchor before acting?

Because wisdom doesn't mean knowing more.

It means knowing what matters most—and why.

Information multiplies.

Wisdom distills.

One adds noise.

The other creates direction.

In the Age of Abundance, the wisest choice isn't to know everything—it's to understand something deeply enough to act on it with peace.

Samuel's words lingered with the group long after that meeting.

They didn't leave with new data—they left with direction.

And that's the point.

Wisdom clears the fog, allowing you to move with intention.

In the next chapter, you'll learn how to put this into motion—how to translate thought into execution through rhythm, reflection, and strategy.

Because wisdom without action is insight unspent.

PART V
K: KEEP MOVING —
THINK → ACT → THRIVE

CHAPTER 13
STRATEGY OVER SPEED

The human brain wasn't designed to move this fast.

Yet here we are—sprinting through days that feel like seconds.

Running a meeting while replying to emails, while half-listening to a podcast on "how to be more productive."

We eat while scrolling.

We walk while typing.

We consume information like oxygen and wonder why we're always out of breath.

We tell ourselves it's multitasking. Optimization. Getting ahead.

But deep down, we know what it really is.

It's panic wearing a smartwatch. It's fear disguised as focus.

We move faster not because we're progressing, but because we're afraid to stop—afraid that if we slow down, we'll feel how lost we really are.

We chase clarity by adding more—more tools, more hacks, more tabs open in our minds—until our thoughts are fragmented across twenty unfinished to-dos and fifty half-read articles.

We call it productivity.

But it's really paralysis in motion.

Somewhere between automation, acceleration, and ambition, we forgot something sacred:

Thinking—our most human act—takes time.

No algorithm can replicate it.

No shortcut can replace it.

And yet we treat it like a luxury instead of what it is: our lifeline.

We've become so focused on keeping up that we've stopped catching up—with ourselves.

That's why this chapter exists.

Thinking, when done well, is not passive or idle.

It's a discipline, a rebellion, a performance art of the soul.

True strategy is what separates **busyness from brilliance.**

Ravi's Reckoning: When Progress Becomes Performance

Ravi's calendar was packed, notifications constant, and his dashboards glowed like a control tower.

He was moving fast—too fast—yet felt strangely disconnected from any real outcome.

That Friday, an AI tool congratulated him: "Productivity up 27% this week!"

He stared at the screen, feeling... empty.

He'd replied to hundreds of emails, managed multiple projects, and consumed mountains of data.

But when he asked himself what truly moved forward, he couldn't name a single thing that mattered.

"I'm exhausted," he admitted, "and somehow still behind."

That's when Samuel's voice echoed in his mind:

"Ravi, if everything matters a little, nothing matters enough."

In that moment, he realized he wasn't managing time; he was mismanaging thought.

The Cognitive Cost of Speed

Harvard Business Review summarized it well:

"Speed kills strategy."

Neuroscientist Daniel Levitin found that constant multitasking floods the brain with cortisol and adrenaline— the stress hormones that impair logic and creativity.

MIT Sloan research shows that teams under "speed pressure" make 40% more short-term decisions with negative long-term outcomes.

In other words: when everything is urgent, nothing is important.

Speed may give the illusion of productivity but robs us of perspective.

And perspective is where wisdom resides.

Microsoft: The Power of Strategic Patience

When Satya Nadella became CEO of Microsoft in 2014, the company was drowning in its own success.

They were shipping products faster than they could stabilize them, competing internally instead of collaborating, and optimizing for quarterly speed rather than long-term significance.

Microsoft was everywhere but not focused anywhere.

Nadella didn't start by urging innovation.

He began by telling people to **breathe.**

He dismantled toxic internal competition, eliminated overlapping initiatives, and reintroduced one simple, radical idea:

"Empathy is our edge."

He encouraged engineers and executives alike to pause before launching anything and ask:

"Who does this serve? What problem does this actually solve? Why does it matter?"

He shifted the company's rhythm from "ship fast" to "learn deeply," from "prove your point" to "expand your understanding."

By slowing the culture down, he created conditions for creative acceleration.

Within a few years, Microsoft had reinvented itself—not through hustle, but through **humility.**

And that's the paradox of progress:

Sometimes the fastest way forward is to slow down enough to see clearly.

Samuel's Conversation

One afternoon, Ravi shared his frustration with Samuel.

"I have a thousand good ideas," he said. "I just can't seem to make any of them stick."

Samuel smiled. "Ideas are easy. Rhythm is rare."

He leaned forward. "You don't need more sprints. You need seasons."

That phrase lingered.

"Seasons?" Ravi asked.

"Yes," Samuel said. "Twelve-week seasons. Long enough to build something real. Short enough to stay awake."

The THINK Cycle: 12 Weeks of Intentional Momentum

The THINK Cycle wasn't about getting more done.

It was about getting aligned.

Ravi didn't want another project management system.

He sought a way to bring thought back into motion—a rhythm that allowed him to breathe and build simultaneously.

With Samuel's help, he developed what they called **The THINK Cycle**—12 weeks of deliberate focus designed to retrain the brain to prioritize thinking before acting.

It's not about efficiency; it's about **engagement.**

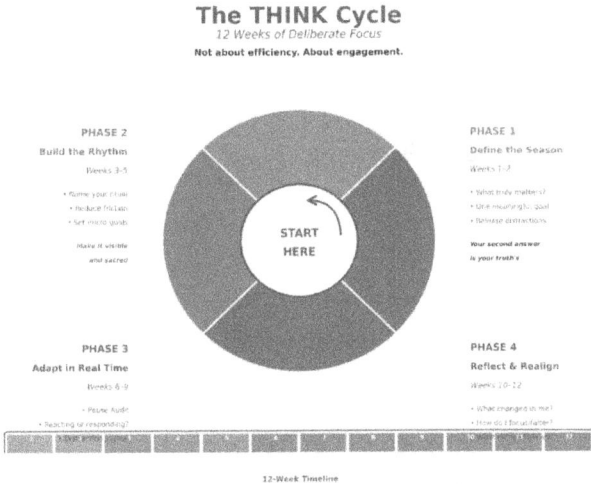

The THINK Cycle
12 Weeks of Deliberate Focus
Not about efficiency. About engagement.

PHASE 2
Build the Rhythm
Weeks 3-5
• Name your ritual
• Reduce friction
• Set micro-goals
Make it visible and sacred

PHASE 1
Define the Season
Weeks 1-2
• What truly matters?
• One meaningful goal
• Release distractions
Your second answer is your truth's

START HERE

PHASE 3
Adapt in Real Time
Weeks 6-9
• Pause: Audit
• Reacting or responding?

PHASE 4
Reflect & Realign
Weeks 10-12
• What changed in me?
• How do I focus better?

12-Week Timeline

Phase 1: Define the Season (Weeks 1–2)

Before pursuing action, cultivate awareness.

Ask yourself:

- What truly matters right now—not in theory, but in truth?
- If I could accomplish only one meaningful thing this quarter, what would it be?
- What distractions am I willing to release to make space for it?

149

Here's the catch:

If you answer these questions too quickly, you're doing it wrong.

Thinking requires slowness.

When you feel the urge to "just get through it," pause.

Write your answers, then sit in silence.

Ask again—and listen deeper.

Your first answer comes from ego; your second reveals your truth.

Phase 2: Build the Rhythm (Weeks 3–5)

Next, design your cadence.

Every week needs an anchor—a ritual that safeguards your thinking space.

For Ravi, it was Sunday mornings: coffee, quiet, notebook open.

For Maya, it was Wednesday afternoons—a no-meeting window she used to review her direction.

Whatever your rhythm is, make it visible and sacred.

Tips to stay on track:

- **Name your rhythm**—assign it an identity ("My Sunday Reset," "The Friday Frame"). Naming gives meaning.
- **Reduce friction**—prepare your tools, notes, and space in advance. Thinking hates clutter.
- **Set micro-goals**—focus on one step, not ten. Progress builds trust with yourself.

Phase 3: Adapt in Real Time (Weeks 6–9)

This is where distractions will fight back.

Rationalizations will creep in: "I'll catch up next week." "I know what I'm doing; I don't need to reflect today."

Don't believe it. That's drift disguised as confidence.

When this happens, use what Samuel called a "Pause Audit." Take two minutes and ask:

"Am I reacting or responding right now?"

If you're reacting, stop. Step away. Recalibrate.

If you're responding—proceed, but stay aware.

Practical trick:

Keep a Distraction Journal—a small notepad or notes app to jot down what pulls your attention.

Patterns will reveal themselves.

Phase 4: Reflect and Realign (Weeks 10–12)

This final phase is where thinking transforms into wisdom.

Here, slow down again—not to end, but to integrate.

Ask:

- What changed—in me, not just in my results?
- What did I learn about how I focus, falter, or flourish?
- What needs to carry forward into the next cycle?

Don't rush this either.

Feeling resistance here is normal.

It means growth is occurring beneath the surface.

Give yourself grace to THINK without producing—that's when insights emerge that no algorithm could generate.

Why Most People Drift Through the THINK Cycle

Samuel once said, "Most people don't fail because they lack a plan.

They fail because they lack presence."

That's the real test.

You can complete the prompts, make the planner look neat, and hit your milestones—and still miss the point.

Because the THINK Cycle isn't about what you finish; it's about how fully you show up to what you start.

If you find yourself rushing through reflections just to check a box, stop. You're doing it again.

When you start to drift, return to this question:

"Am I thinking—or just moving?"

If the answer is "just moving," pause.

That pause is your power.

Faith, Focus, and the Future

The THINK Cycle works because it mirrors something deeply spiritual: rhythm, rest, and reflection.

We see it in nature—the tides, the seasons, the breath.

Creation itself moves in cycles, not sprints.

Neuroscience confirms this: creativity and problem-solving peak not during intense work, but during structured mental rest (Stanford, 2020).

Faith—whether spiritual or simply a belief in process—invites you to trust that rhythm.

It encourages you to believe that what's growing underground still matters, even when you can't see it.

To trust that growth is happening, even when it appears stagnant above.

Thinking operates similarly. You may not see immediate results, but something essential is forming: wisdom, clarity, resilience.

Reflection: Redeeming Your Rhythm

- Where are you confusing motion with meaning?
- What rhythm—daily, weekly, or seasonal—could help you slow down enough to THINK clearly?
- What do you need to protect your focus from—distraction, comparison, or hurry?
- How could you honor thinking not as a task, but as an act of faith?

Speed is loud.

Strategy is quiet.

Thinking is sacred.

When you learn to move at the pace of purpose, you stop performing for the world and start participating in it.

CHAPTER 14
FAITH IN MOTION

When You Don't See the Path, Walk Anyway

It was 2 a.m., and Lena stared at her laptop, the cursor blinking like a heartbeat she couldn't match.

Her latest campaign—the one built with new frameworks, AI tools, and careful strategy—had flopped.

Engagement was down. Clients were frustrated. The data was cold.

She had done everything "right," followed every rule, and still, it hadn't worked.

That's when the old voice returned—the one she thought she'd outgrown.

"You're not keeping up." "You've lost your edge." "Maybe you were never really that good."

The inner critic doesn't shout; it whispers—just enough to sound familiar.

That's what makes it dangerous.

The Weight of the Word "Failure"

Failure has a sound.

It's the quiet click of "refresh" on your analytics page.

It's the silence after sharing something meaningful and receiving no response.

But failure's true power lies in the story you tell yourself about it.

What hurts isn't always the outcome; it's the interpretation.

We replay the same tired scripts:

"I'm not ready." "I'm not enough." "I always mess this up."

These stories aren't truths; they're habits—old mental paradigms your brain clings to because familiarity feels safer than freedom.

But what if failure isn't a verdict?

What if it's just a feedback loop—a mirror showing you what you're ready to refine?

Dyson's 5,000 Prototypes

James Dyson built 5,127 prototypes before he found one that worked.

Five thousand times, he tested, adjusted, and began again.

When asked how he handled frustration, he said:

"Every failure was a step closer. Each mistake was information."

Dyson didn't view failure as evidence of inadequacy.

He considered it a conversation with reality.

That's what true thinkers do.

They listen to feedback without succumbing to self-judgment.

They rewrite the narrative.

Instead of thinking, "This means I can't," they consider,

"This means I'm learning what doesn't work—and that's progress."

Psychologist Carol Dweck refers to this as the growth mindset—the belief that ability isn't fixed but developed through effort, strategy, and feedback.

Those who embrace this mindset not only persist longer but also learn faster.

Faith in motion operates similarly.

It doesn't mean believing everything will go smoothly.

It means trusting that even when things go awry, something meaningful is still unfolding.

Samuel's Lesson: The Story Beneath the Story

When Lena met with Samuel the next morning, she expected strategies.

Instead, he handed her a notebook.

"Write down everything your failure is telling you," he said. "All the thoughts, judgments, and fears."

She frowned. "Isn't that just wallowing?"

Samuel smiled. "No. It's awareness. You can't rewrite a story you refuse to acknowledge."

So she wrote:

"I'm not relevant."

"Everyone's ahead of me."

"I peaked years ago."

When she finished, Samuel pointed to the page.

"Now, cross out what's not true."

Lena hesitated—then slowly drew a line through each sentence.

"That's the work," he said softly. "That's thinking. That's faith. You can't control the feedback life gives you—but you can control the frame you place around it."

Modern psychology supports this. Researchers at UCLA found that simply labeling your thoughts—naming them without judgment—reduces the intensity of negative emotion in the brain's amygdala.

Awareness, not avoidance, initiates healing.

The Power of Reframing

Most people never learn to reframe. They interpret experiences through the lens of old narratives—stories shaped by childhood, early jobs, and the need to prove themselves.

But reframing is how you transition from shame to strategy.

Instead of saying, "This failed because I'm bad at this," you ask, "What is this failure revealing about what I didn't yet know?"

Instead of, "This means I can't," you say, "This means I've found another variable to improve."

Faith transforms pain into progress.

It asks, "What could this mean if I stopped assuming the worst?"

That question rewires the brain's prediction model—the part that constantly forecasts threats. Choosing curiosity over catastrophe allows your brain to update its map of possibilities.

Leaders who practice this create psychological safety—the condition that Harvard's Amy Edmondson identified as the strongest predictor of high-performing teams. Environments that normalize iteration—not perfection—foster innovation and trust.

Faith, then, isn't denial. It is disciplined interpretation.

The Fear of Stagnation

Samuel later shared a profound truth:

"Fear loves stillness—not the sacred kind, but the stuck kind."

Fear thrives on inertia. The longer you hesitate, the louder it becomes.

When you move—even clumsily, even slowly—you break the illusion that failure defines you.

Because faith doesn't eliminate fear; it dilutes it—with action, learning, and truth.

Movement is the antidote to mental paralysis.

Tiny Tactic: 5-minute rule. Commit to five minutes on the next step. Getting started shrinks fear; momentum takes care of the rest.

Faith as a Cognitive Skill

Faith isn't mystical; it's neurological.

When you act—when you try again—you literally rewire the brain's narrative center, shifting from the **default mode network** (rumination and replay) to the **executive network** (creation and focus).

You stop reinforcing "I failed" and start teaching your brain, "I'm adapting."

That's **neuroplasticity**—the brain's ability to reorganize itself through experience. Every time you choose curiosity over criticism, you carve new pathways.

Psychologist Peter Gollwitzer's research on implementation intentions illustrates this: when people link a trigger to an action—"If X happens, I will Y"—follow-through rates double.

In this sense, faith is a cognitive plan for courage.

Your neurons grasp it perfectly.

Iteration as Identity

Faith in motion means making iteration your identity.

You're not someone who occasionally fails; you're someone who is becoming through feedback.

Lena eventually realized her campaign wasn't a failure—it was a signal.

It highlighted where her thinking had plateaued and reminded her that success isn't about flawless execution—it's about consistent interpretation.

So she reframed again:

"This didn't work—and that's working for me."

Every setback, viewed through a renewed mind, becomes a stepping stone.

How to Rewrite the Story in Real Time

Samuel taught his team a simple three-step reset—a method to intercept old mental loops before they take hold:

1. Notice the Narrative. When something goes wrong, catch the story forming in your head.

("I always mess this up." "Nothing I do works.")

2. Name the Lesson. Ask, "What is this trying to show me?"

Failure doesn't mock you—it mentors you, if you let it.

3. Nudge Forward. Take one meaningful action immediately—send the email, make the call, tweak the prototype.

That motion rewires the narrative.

Each time you do this, you train your brain to replace reaction with reflection—and reflection with resilience.

Pro Tip:

Turn the nudge into an if-then plan (implementation intention): If my post underperforms at 24 hours, then I will interview two customers and iterate the headline and hook.

Resilience as Rhythm

Lena eventually stopped fearing failure because she recognized it as part of her rhythm—an essential feedback loop within the THINK Cycle itself.

It wasn't a detour; it was the design.

Each stumble was data. Each attempt was a draft. Each moment of reflection was a reset.

Faith in motion didn't mean never falling; it meant falling forward—and believing that growth awaited in the fall.

Faith as Movement, Not Motto

Faith isn't about ignoring reality; it's about interpreting it differently.

It's movement guided by meaning.

It's the courage to ask, "What if this setback isn't here to stop me, but to stretch me?"

Faith in motion transforms experience into evolution.

Guardrail: Beware of survivorship bias. Celebrate wins, but study misses with equal curiosity. Both carry information; only one flatters the ego.

Reflection: Rewrite Your Feedback Loop

- What story do you tell yourself when things don't go as planned?
- How can you reframe that narrative to empower growth?
- Where are you confusing feedback with failure?
- What small act of movement can help you replace fear with faith right now?

Failure isn't final.
Feedback isn't personal.
And faith isn't still.

When you rewrite the story, you transform the self.

And when you move with faith—even imperfectly—you discover what every great thinker, creator, and leader eventually learns:

Progress is born not from perfection, but from permission—the permission to begin again.

CHAPTER 15
THE IRREPLACEABLE HUMAN

Closing the Loop—Where Thought Becomes Legacy

The air inside the small meeting room hummed with quiet anticipation.

It had been nearly a year since Lena, Ravi, and Maya first crossed paths in Samuel's workshops—a year since they each reached their breaking points and learned to rebuild with rhythm, clarity, and courage.

Now, they sat together for the first time since their separate journeys began.

Though their stories had diverged, their discoveries converged into something shared:

The realization that thinking wasn't a skill; it was a calling.

The Gathering

Samuel stood at the front of the room, hands clasped loosely, eyes kind yet alert.

He didn't need to command attention; his presence did that for him.

"Before we begin," he said, "I want you to look around this room. You're witnessing proof of what's possible when people choose to THINK instead of drift."

Lena smiled faintly.

Ravi leaned forward.

Maya nodded, her notebook open, pages filled with small, deliberate handwriting.

"Each of you faced something that was supposed to break you," Samuel said. "And each of you used it to build a new way of seeing."

He gestured to the whiteboard behind him, where five words were written in steady script:

Think. Harness. Imagine. Navigate. Keep.

The THINK rhythm.

Alive. Lived. Proven.

"This," he continued, "isn't a method. It's a mindset.

A way of navigating a world that's changing faster than anyone can predict."

The Age of Automation

Samuel clicked to the next slide—two simple images side by side.

On one side: a photo of a Blockbuster store, lights dim, windows boarded.

On the other: the Netflix homepage, vibrant with color, stories, and endless motion.

"Two companies looked at the same future," he said. "One defended the status quo. The other imagined what could be."

He clicked again.

BlackBerry beside Apple.

"Two more companies examined the same technology.

One optimized keyboards. The other reimagined touch."

He looked up, voice steady.

"The difference between those who endure and those who disappear isn't resources.

It's reflection."

"Not access. Awareness."

"Not data. Discernment."

He paused. "Thinking—deep, imaginative, intentional thinking—is not what slows progress down.

It's what makes progress possible."

Research supports this: MIT Sloan's 2022 leadership study found that companies emphasizing reflective decision-making outperform reactive ones by 26% in long-term growth.

Reflection, not speed, is what scales clarity.

What the Machines Can't Do

As the conversation began, Ravi spoke first. "AI can do almost everything faster now—code, write, analyze. But it still needs us to tell it what matters."

Maya added, "It can mimic creativity, but it can't feel awe."

Lena smiled softly. "And it can process data—but it can't hold faith."

Samuel nodded.

"Exactly," he said. "Technology can replicate knowledge, but not wisdom. It can automate processes, but not purpose. It can calculate value, but not create meaning."

He looked at them—and, symbolically, at the reader—and continued:

"We don't need to compete with machines.

We need to complete what they can't."

The room fell into thoughtful silence.

As Oxford philosopher Luciano Floridi notes, AI is "semantically competent but **ethically blind.**" It can process symbols but not significance—because meaning arises only from consciousness aware of consequence.

The Human Advantage

Thinking is not an inconvenience.

It's our inheritance.

It's what built every innovation that changed the world—the spark behind every leap forward.

Every breakthrough begins with one human pausing long enough to ask, "What if?"

That's the unreplicable spark of the human mind:

The ability to imagine the unseen, to choose the unseen, and to believe in it long enough to make it real.

AI can process, predict, and even generate—but it cannot decide what is worth doing.

Only a thinking human can do that.

That is our advantage.

And it's time we reclaimed it.

Harvard psychologist Howard Gardner calls this existential intelligence—the ability to ask meaning-making questions. It's not just intellect; it's insight. And it's uniquely, beautifully human.

The Return of the Thinkers

Samuel looked around the room one last time.

"Thinking," he said, "isn't an escape from the future. It's how we design it."

He handed each person a blank notebook. "No prompts this time," he said. "No templates. Just space."

They opened their notebooks and, almost simultaneously, began to write.

Not tasks.

Not plans.

But thoughts.

Lena's first line: 'I am no longer afraid of silence.' Ravi's: 'I am learning to lead through learning.' Maya's: 'I will protect my mind like it's sacred—because it is.'

Samuel smiled. "That," he said quietly, "is how the future is written."

The room fell into stillness—not empty, but alive.

Each pen moved slowly and deliberately, like thought becoming visible.

Modern research confirms what they were feeling: studies from Princeton and UCLA show that writing by hand activates the brain's deeper centers for comprehension, memory, and emotional insight.

Typing captures words; handwriting captures meaning.

Thought flows differently when ink meets paper—slower, more deliberate, more human.

Your Turn

You, reading this now—you're part of that future too.

This book wasn't meant to give you all the answers.

It was meant to reawaken your questions.

You've learned the rhythm: **Truth, Harness, Imagine, Navigate, Keep.**

Now it's time to live it.

When you pause before reacting—you're thinking.

When you choose integrity over convenience—you're thinking.

When you stay curious while fear tells you to freeze—you're thinking.

And every time you THINK, you reassert your humanity in a world that keeps trying to automate it away.

Faith, Imagination, and the Future

The future will not belong to those who memorize the most or move the fastest.

It will belong to those who see clearly, choose bravely, and imagine boldly.

It will belong to those who infuse faith into function, soul into systems, and imagination into innovation.

Because faith without thought is blind.

And thought without faith is hollow.

Together, they create the only equation powerful enough to propel humanity forward.

Philosopher Viktor Frankl wrote, "Between stimulus and response, there is a space. In that space is our power to choose."

That space—the pause, the reflection, the trust in our own agency—is where the irreplaceable human resides.

Your Invitation

You don't need to build an AI company or launch a movement to make a difference.

You just need to become unshakably aware of your thoughts, your gifts, and your ability to choose meaning over noise.

Every significant change begins the same way:

With one person, somewhere, deciding to THINK differently.

That's where your journey continues.

This book ends here, but the practice—your rhythm, your awareness, your faith—begins now.

Because thinking isn't just how you survive the future.

It's how you author it.

The future isn't automated.

It's authored—by thinkers like you.

EPILOGUE

THE CONVERSATION
THAT STARTED IT ALL

It began, as so many turning points do, in an ordinary moment.

A couch.

A quiet evening.

A conversation with my father-in-law, Jim—a man who built a life the old-fashioned way: hard work, long days, and the steady rhythm of doing what needed to be done.

He looked at me that night—eyes filled with both wisdom and worry—and asked,

"What's going to happen to people when all of this—" he waved at the news of automation and AI "—takes over? How will anyone build a career anymore?"

I didn't have the answer then.

But I felt the weight of the question.

Jim wasn't afraid for himself.

He was concerned for those coming after—his grandkids, his great-grandkids, people like you and me trying to make sense of a world moving at the speed of code.

That question—how do we stay human in the age of machines? —planted the seed for this book.

The Years Between

I've lived a dozen lives since then.

An engineer who learned to see systems.

A marketer who learned to tell stories.

An entrepreneur who learned to build from nothing.

And in every season, I sought the same thing: how to THINK my way through change instead of merely reacting to it.

Then, a few years ago, I began working with a coach named Nancy Kirkham, who changed everything.

Nancy didn't teach me how to plan or perform.

She taught me how to **THINK.**

To stop equating activity with progress.

To question the narratives in my mind.

To slow down long enough to hear my own thoughts again.

That's when I began to see it clearly: thinking wasn't something we did; it was something we'd forgotten how to honor.

And that forgetting is what makes us replaceable—not technology.

The True Crisis

The real crisis of our age isn't automation.

It's **mental autopilot.**

It's the drift—the slow slide into allowing algorithms, headlines, and busyness to THINK for us.

That's why this book isn't just about AI.

It's about awakening.

When you begin to THINK intentionally again—choosing awareness over automation, curiosity over comfort, and creation over consumption—you become irreplaceable.

Not because of what you know, but because of how you see.

The Thread That Runs Through It All

Jim's question still echoes in my mind.

Nancy's voice continues to guide my thoughts.

Every day, I watch the world accelerate and remind myself:

the future isn't determined by those who move fastest, but by those who THINK deepest.

That's why I wrote this—not to add noise to an already loud world, but to provide silence, space, and structure for what matters most.

If You Remember One Thing

If you remember one thing from this book, let it be this:

You are not behind.

You are not too late.

You are not replaceable.

You are a thinker—a creator, a designer of meaning in a world that craves it.

Every time you pause to THINK—to question, to imagine, to believe—you reclaim your place in the story of what's next.

In the end, no algorithm can dream what you can dream.

No machine can hold the kind of faith that fuels human progress.

And no system can replicate the sacred act of a mind choosing to THINK freely.

AFTERWORD
FOR THINKERS

A Letter from Annabelen:

If you've made it this far, I want to pause—and thank you.

Not for reading, but for thinking. For giving yourself the rare gift of reflection in a world addicted to reaction.

This book wasn't meant to be the final word.

It was meant to be a beginning—a spark.

A reminder that your thoughts have power, and that power multiplies when shared.

We are entering an era where our greatest competitive advantage is no longer speed, data, or even skill—it's depth.

Depth of thought.

Depth of imagination.

Depth of humanity.

That's what this movement—the THINK Movement—is about.

It's a growing community of individuals who refuse to drift.

Leaders. Creators. Dreamers. Engineers. Entrepreneurs.

People just like you—who want to live with more clarity, courage, and consciousness.

Together, we explore how to apply these principles—not just in business, but in life.

Through workshops. Newsletters. Private sessions. Conversations that slow the noise and sharpen your focus.

The future won't be built by those who memorize trends.

It will be built by those who make meaning.

If that's you—and I believe it is—I invite you to stay connected.

Join the THINK community—where we keep learning how to THINK deeply, lead intentionally, and live awake.

You can find me at thinkingedge.online or by subscribing to the THINK Letter, a monthly reflection on purpose, imagination, and the future of work and life.

Thank you for thinking with me.

Thank you for choosing awareness over automation.

And thank you for helping to bring back the one thing this world needs most—humans who still THINK for themselves.

Keep thinking.

Keep choosing.

Keep becoming.

With gratitude,
Annabelen Hemelgarn

ACKNOWLEDGMENTS

To my husband, John—thank you for your unwavering patience and endless support throughout my entrepreneurial journey. You've been my steady anchor during late nights, bold ideas, and periods of growth. I couldn't have done this without your love and belief in me.

To my family—thank you for granting me grace during long hours, tight deadlines, and the chaos that often accompanies building something from the ground up. Your understanding and encouragement have meant everything.

To my father-in-law, Jim—your influence has been the heartbeat of this book. You reminded me why this work matters and inspired me to articulate my thoughts.

To my coaches and mentors—especially Nancy—thank you for sharing your wisdom, challenging my perspectives, and helping me cultivate the awareness that has shaped both my business and my life.

And to the great thinkers who came before me—Napoleon Hill, Carol Dweck, and countless others whose words have influenced my thinking—thank you for lighting the path.

This book reflects that continuous journey—to keep reading, growing, and above all, *thinking*.

ABOUT THE AUTHOR

Annabelen Hemelgarn is a strategist, trainer, and entrepreneur who helps leaders THINK differently in an age of automation and constant change. A Purdue-trained engineer turned digital marketer and founder of multiple seven-figure businesses, she's built her career on curiosity, courage, and a steadfast belief that human thinking—not technology—is our greatest strength.

As the creator of **The THINK Framework**, Annabelen blends strategy, neuroscience, and faith to guide others in slowing down, thinking deeply, and leading with intention through transformation.

But her most meaningful discovery came when she realized that the real threat to our future isn't automation—it's mental autopilot. That insight led to the birth of The THINK Framework, a system designed to help leaders, entrepreneurs, and organizations think with clarity, creativity, and faith in a world changing faster than ever.

When she's not teaching or speaking about authentic intelligence, Annabelen leads her digital agency—helping entrepreneurs reclaim their time, scale their businesses, and harness AI in ways that enhance both efficiency and humanity.

Beyond her work, Annabelen's proudest role has always been family. Though her six children are now grown, she continues to pour her heart into guiding their journeys and inspiring her grandchildren to live with purpose, creativity, and heart.

Through her workshops, speaking engagements, and the growing THINK Platform, she equips others to move from reactive to intentional—from drifting to designing their future—all while reminding them that true intelligence begins with reflection, not reaction.

Learn more at thinkingedge.online.

And don't forget to scan the QR code and download your book resources: